101

best campsites

for **you** & **your dog**

2014

alan rogers

Compiled by: **Alan Rogers Travel Ltd**

Designed by: **Vine Design Ltd**

© Alan Rogers Travel Ltd 2013

Published by: **Alan Rogers Travel Ltd,**
Spelmonden Old Oast, Goudhurst, Kent TN17 1HE
Tel: **01580 214000** www.alanrogers.com

British Library Cataloguing-in-Publication Data:
A catalogue record for this book is
available from the British Library.

ISBN 978-1-909057-32-6

Printed in Great Britain by
Stephens & George Print Group

Contents

Welcome to the Alan Rogers
'101' guides

The Alan Rogers guides have been helping campers and caravanners make informed decisions about their holiday destinations since 1968. Today, whether online or in print, Alan Rogers still provides an independent, impartial view, with detailed reports, on each campsite.

With so much unfiltered, unqualified information freely available, the Alan Rogers perspective is invaluable to make sure you make the right choice for your holiday.

What is the
'101' series?

At Alan Rogers, we know that readers have many and diverse interests, hobbies and particular requirements. And we know that our guides, featuring a total of some 3,000 campsites, can provide a bewildering choice from which it can be difficult to produce a shortlist of possible holiday destinations.

The Alan Rogers 101 guides are devised as a means of presenting a realistic, digestible number of great campsites, featured because of their suitability to a given theme.

This book remains first and foremost an authoritative guide to excellent campsites which go out of their way to make dogs welcome and make holidaying with your dog just a little easier.

101 Best campsites
for you and your dog

Campsites have wide-ranging policies and rules on dogs and this can sometimes be confusing.

However, the good news for those heading abroad, is that taking your dog with you has become simpler and more painless as procedures have been clarified.

This guide identifies 101 great campsites that welcome dogs, both in the UK and on the continent. They may have certain restrictions (e.g. regarding dates, breeds, sizes and so on) so you are advised to check with the campsite directly regarding your own specific plans.

There are 101 wonderful campsites in this guide, in a wide range of styles and locations, so you are sure to find your ideal holiday destination here.

Alan Rogers – in search
of 'the best'

Alan Rogers himself started off with the very specific aim of providing people with the necessary information to allow them to make an informed decision about their holiday destination. Today we still do that with a range of guides that now covers Europe's best campsites in 27 countries. We work with campsites all day, every day. We visit campsites for inspection purposes (or even just for pleasure!). We know campsites 'inside out'.

We know which campsites would suit active families; which are great for get-away-from-it-all couples; we know which campsites are planning super new pool complexes; which campsites offer a fantastic menu in their on-site restaurant; which campsites allow you to launch a small boat from their slipway; which campsites have a decent playing area for kicking a ball around; which campsites have flat, grassy pitches and which have solid hardstandings.

We also know which are good for fishing, children, nature and outdoor activities; which are close to the beach; and which welcome dogs. These particular themes form our '101' series.

All Alan Rogers guides (and our website) are respected for their independent, impartial and honest assessment. The reviews are prose-based, without overuse of indecipherable icons and symbols.
Our simple aim is to help guide you to a campsite that best matches your requirements – often quite difficult in today's age of information overload.

What is
the best?

The criteria we use when inspecting and selecting sites are numerous, but the most important by far is the question of good quality. People want different things from their choice of campsite, so campsite 'styles' vary dramatically: from small peaceful campsites in the heart of the countryside, to 'all singing, all dancing' sites in popular seaside resorts.

The size of the site, whether it's part of a chain or privately owned, makes no difference in terms of it being required to meet our exacting standards in respect of its quality and it being 'fit for purpose'. In other words, irrespective of the size of the site, or the number of facilities it offers, we consider and evaluate the welcome, the pitches, the sanitary facilities, the cleanliness, the general maintenance and even the location.

Expert
opinions

We rely on our dedicated team of Site Assessors, all of whom are experienced campers, caravanners or motorcaravanners, to visit and recommend campsites. Each year they travel around Europe inspecting new campsites for Alan Rogers and re-inspecting the existing ones.

When planning
your holiday...

A holiday should always be a relaxing affair, and a campsite-based holiday particularly so. Our aim is for you to find the ideal campsite for your holiday, one that suits your requirements. All Alan Rogers guides provide a wealth of information, including some details supplied by campsite owners themselves, and the following points may help ensure that you plan a successful holiday.

Find out more

An Alan Rogers reference number (eg FR12345) is given for each campsite and can be useful for finding more information and pictures online at www.alanrogers.com. Simply enter this number in the 'Campsite Search' field on the Home page.

Campsite descriptions

We aim to convey an idea of its general appearance, 'feel' and features, with details of pitch numbers, electricity, hardstandings etc.

Facilities

We list specific information on the site's facilities and amenities and, where available, the dates when these facilities are open (if not for the whole season). Much of this information is as supplied to us and may be subject to change. Should any particular activity or aspect of the campsite be important to you, it is always worth discussing with the campsite before you travel.

Swimming pools

Opening dates, any charges and levels of supervision are provided where we have been notified. In some countries (notably France) there is a regulation whereby Bermuda-style shorts may not be worn in swimming pools (for health and hygiene reasons). It is worth ensuring that you do take 'proper' swimming trunks with you.

Charges

Those given are the latest provided to us, usually 2013 prices, and should be viewed as a guide only.

Toilet blocks

Unless we comment otherwise, toilet blocks will be equipped with a reasonable number of British style WCs, washbasins and hot showers in cubicles. We also assume that there will be an identified chemical toilet disposal point, and that the campsite will provide water and waste water drainage points and bin areas. If not the case, we comment. We do mention certain features that some readers find important: washbasins in cubicles, facilities for babies, facilities for those with disabilities and motorcaravan service points.

Reservations

Necessary for high season (roughly mid-July to mid-August) in popular holiday areas (i.e. beach resorts). You can reserve many sites via our own Alan Rogers Travel Service or through other tour operators. Remember, many sites are closed all winter and you may struggle to get an answer.

Telephone numbers

All numbers assume that you are phoning from within the country in question. From the UK or Ireland, dial 00, then the country's prefix (e.g. France is 33), then the campsite number given, but dropping the first '0'.

Opening dates

Dates given are those provided to us and can alter before the start of the season. If you intend to visit shortly after a published opening date, or shortly before the closing date, it is wise to check that it will actually be open at the time required. Similarly some sites operate a restricted service during the low season, only opening some of their facilities (e.g. swimming pools) during the main season; where we know about this, and have the relevant dates, we indicate it; again if you are at all doubtful it is wise to check.

Accommodation

Over recent years, more and more campsites have added high quality mobile homes, chalets, lodges, gîtes and more. Where applicable we indicate what is available and you'll find details online.

Special Offers

Some campsites have taken the opportunity to highlight a special offer. This is arranged by them and for clarification please contact the campsite direct.

Dog days
# of summer

Camping holidays offer a wonderful opportunity to enjoy some real 'r and r' without leaving your beloved dog behind; a change of scene, different routines, lots of fresh air will benefit everyone, whether with two legs or four. And since 3rd July 2004, with a PETS (Pet Travel Scheme) passport, your dog can enjoy a continental camping holiday just as much as you.

Dogs
on campsites

Campsites are all about enjoying the freedom of the fresh air, wonderful scenery and a relaxed lifestyle, away from the usual routines of home. Of course, dogs can benefit from all this too! In addition they enjoy new walks, new smells and the affectionate attention of friendly passers by. They are, however, perhaps less interested in the cultural sights!

Basic rules
& etiquette

On the continent, dogs are generally far more welcome in shops and restaurants than in the UK. A well behaved dog sitting beside the table in a restaurant is by no means uncommon.

Of course, each site has different rules so be sure to check before you book – for example, some campsites have restrictions on breeds and sizes of dog permitted. But no matter how well trained and obedient they may be, certain basic rules generally apply.

- Expect to be required to keep your dog on a lead
- Respect others *(it may be hard to imagine, but some people do not like or are afraid of dogs)*
- Don't fall out with the campsite owner, keep barking to a minimum
- Be sure to clean up after your dog

In return, you will find on many dog-friendly sites certain measures are in place to make a dog's life that little bit more pleasurable. You may find a special area set aside for exercising dogs, or perhaps a path where an evening stroll becomes a pleasant after dinner ritual. Provision of washing stations, or dog showers, are not unheard of and even on-site dog classes have been known.

Taking your
dog abroad

Travelling long distances in hot summer conditions can be dangerous for dogs. Dogs control body temperature mainly by panting. In fact, signs to look out for are abnormally heavy panting, agitated activity and perhaps whining. The dog may produce more drooling saliva than normal, and eyes may become glassy. Treat overheating promptly: find a cool shaded place, offer drinking water and spray the dog with cool water.

The pet
passport

Of course with so many great campsites to choose from across Europe, you may be planning to head abroad. However, pet travel rules changed on 1 January 2012, when the UK brought its procedures into line with the European Union. From this date, all pets can enter or re-enter the UK from any country in the world without quarantine provided they meet the rules of the Pet Travel Scheme, which will be different depending on the country or territory the pet is coming from.

Your dog must:

- Be fitted with a microchip
  (to assist identification on a national database)

- Be vaccinated against rabies
  (vaccination will not count if your dog has not been microchipped first)

- Be accompanied either by a pet passport or an official third country veterinary certificate

- Be treated against tapeworm

You are required to wait 21 days from the date of the first rabies vaccination before travelling.

In some circumstances (for 'unlisted' countries), after your dog has been vaccinated, it must be blood tested (to ensure satisfactory effect of the rabies vaccination), and must wait 3 months from the date of the blood test before travelling.

Treatment against tapeworm should be carried out not less than 24 hours and not more than 120 hours (1-5 days) before returning to the UK. The vet will stamp the pet passport and record the time and date of treatment.

Travel must be with an authorised carrier, using an approved route.

Please refer to the following website for full details on taking your dog abroad. www.gov.uk/take-pet-abroad

Forward planning is crucial – best start at least 8 months before you plan to travel.

What will it cost me?

Exact costs will vary but you can expect to pay between £120 and £160 per dog (including microchipping, rabies jab, blood test, issuing of pet passport). A vet's fee in France might cost around £20, excluding treatments. Ferry companies usually charge £30-£60 each way to take your dog.

It's a
dog's life

If crossing the Channel expect your dog to remain in the vehicle on short crossings. On longer crossings dogs may be moved to on board kennels, with provision for accompanied visits. For first time or nervous dogs, you may wish to cross the Channel with Eurotunnel, allowing you to travel with your dog in the vehicle.

On the ferry
tips

- Check in early – makes for a relaxed check in
- Choose a short crossing
  (e.g. to Calais or Dunkirk)
- Consider travelling overnight, when the
  temperature is cooler
- When boarding, ensure the officials know that
  you have a dog in the vehicle
- When leaving your vehicle, make sure that your
  dog has adequate ventilation
- Make sure your dog has drinking water

Fit
to travel

Some tips to help make your dog's journey as comfortable as possible:

- Provide a light meal about two hours before they travel
- Allow your dog the chance to go to the toilet before setting off
- If travelling in a container, allow your dog to familiarise itself
  with it in advance
- Bring a familiar smelling cushion or rug to help your dog settle
- Obvious, perhaps, but plenty of ventilation, shade and fresh drinking
  water are essential
- It is worth checking the regulations for the country you are visiting as
  some countries insist that dogs wear canine seat belts or be carried
  in a cage
- Make sure your dog wears an identification collar and tag
  with your current contact details

Pet Insurance

You wouldn't travel without insurance for yourself, so a good pet insurance
policy that covers your dog while you're away offers peace of mind.

Assistance Dogs

If travelling with an assistance dog, consult Defra and your ferry company.

Enjoy...!

Whether you're an 'old hand' or are contemplating your first trip, a regular reader of our Guides or a new 'convert', we wish you well in your travels and hope we have been able to help in some way. We are, of course, also out and about ourselves, visiting sites, talking to owners and readers, and generally checking on standards and new developments. We hope to bump into you!

Wishing you thoroughly enjoyable camping and caravanning in 2014 – favoured by good weather of course!

The Alan Rogers Team

Useful
websites

This is primarily a guide to excellent dog friendly campsites and does not set out to be a definitive explanation of your legal obligations. Please check your own requirements well in advance.

www.gov.uk/defra – *follow the link for taking your pet abroad*

www.bva.co.uk – *British Veterinary Association*

www.dogsaway.co.uk – *Vastly experienced specialists in ensuring welfare and peace of mind when travelling with dogs*

www.pethealthcouncil.co.uk – *Health issues*

www.apbc.org.uk – *Association of Pet Behaviour Counsellors*

Facilities: Toilet blocks of a very high standard include some en-suite showers with basins. Good facilities for disabled visitors. Washing machines. Gas supplies. Excellent supermarket. Restaurants, pizzeria and bar. Two separate bars and snack bar by beach where discos are held in main season. Sailing, diving and windsurfing schools. 300 sq.m. swimming pool. Tennis courts. Squash. Paddle court. Fronton. Minigolf. Games room. Riding tuition (July/Aug). Children's play park and miniclub. Fishing (licence required). Car, motorcycle and bicycle hire. Hairdresser. Internet access and WiFi over site (charged). ATM. Torches are useful near beach.
Off site: Canal trips 18 km. Aquatic Park 20 km.

Open: 11 May - 15 September (with all services).

Directions: Site is signed at 26 km. marker on C252 between Castello d'Empúries and Vildemat, then 7 km. to site. Alternatively, on San Pescador-Castello d'Empúries road (GIV6261) head north and site is well signed.

GPS: 42.206077, 3.10389

Charges guide

Per unit incl. 2 persons and electricity	€ 30,70 - € 61,45
extra person (over 3 yrs)	€ 3,15 - € 5,75
dog	€ 5,35 - € 6,90
boat or jet ski	€ 10,30 - € 13,50

Spain – Castelló d'Empúries

Camping Nautic Almata

Ctra GIV- 6216 km 2,3, E-17486 Castelló d'Empúries (Girona)
t: 972 454 477   e: info@almata.com
alanrogers.com/ES80300   www.almata.com

Accommodation: ◉ Pitch ◉ Mobile home/chalet ○ Hotel/B&B ○ Apartment

In the Bay of Roses, south of Empuriabrava and beside the Parc Natural dels Aiguamolls de l'Empordá, this is a high quality site of particular interest to nature lovers (especially birdwatchers). A large site, there are 1,109 well kept, large, numbered pitches, all with electricity and on flat, sandy ground. Beautifully laid out, it is arranged around the river and waterways, so will suit those who like to be close to water or who enjoy watersports and boating. It is also a superb beachside site. There are some pitches right on the beach and on the banks of the canal. As you drive through the nature park to the site, enjoy the wild flamingos alongside the road. The name no doubt derives from the fact that boats can be tied up at the small marina within the site and a slipway also gives access to a river and thence to the sea. Throughout the season there is a varied entertainment programme for children and adults, and the facilities are impressive. Tour operators use the site.

You might like to know

There are some excellent walks in the vicinity of the campsite. Dogs are free of charge here in low season.

- ◉ Dogs welcome *(subject to conditions)*
- ◉ Dogs welcome all season
- ○ Dogs welcome part season
- ◉ Breed restrictions *(e.g. only small dogs accepted)*
- ◉ Number restrictions *(max. 1 or 2 dogs)*
- ○ Dog sanitary facilities *(e.g. waste bins, bags)*
- ○ Dog showers
- ○ On-site dog walking area
- ○ Kennels
- ○ Vet nearby *(able to help with UK Pet Passports)*

Camping Las Dunas

Ctra San Marti-Sant Pere, E-17470 Sant Pere Pescador (Girona)
t: 972 521 717   e: info@campinglasdunas.com
alanrogers.com/ES80400   www.campinglasdunas.com

Accommodation: ☑ Pitch ☑ Mobile home/chalet ○ Hotel/B&B ○ Apartment

Las Dunas is an extremely large, impressive and well organised resort-style site with many on-site activities and an ongoing programme of improvements. It has direct access to a superb sandy beach that stretches along the site for nearly a kilometre with a windsurfing school and beach bar. There is also a much used, huge swimming pool, plus a large double pool for children. Las Dunas is very large, with 1,700 individual hedged pitches (1,500 for touring units) of around 100 sq.m. laid out on flat ground in long, regular parallel rows. All have electricity (6/10A) and 180 also have water and drainage. Shade is available in some parts of the site. Pitches are usually available, even in the main season. Much effort has gone into planting palms and new trees here and the results are very attractive. The large restaurant and bar have spacious terraces overlooking the swimming pools or you can enjoy a very pleasant, more secluded, cavern-style pub. A magnificent disco club is close by in a soundproofed building (although people returning from this during the night can be a problem for pitches in the central area of the site). A member of Leading Campings group.

Facilities: Five excellent large toilet blocks with electronic sliding glass doors (resident cleaners 07.00-21.00). British style toilets but no seats, controllable hot showers and washbasins in cabins. Excellent facilities for youngsters, babies and disabled campers. Laundry facilities. Motorcaravan services. Extensive supermarket, boutique and other shops. Large bar with terrace. Large restaurant. New takeaway and terrace in 2012. Ice cream parlour. Beach bar in main season. Disco club. Swimming pools. Playgrounds. Tennis. Archery. Minigolf. Sailing/windsurfing school and other watersports. Programme of sports, games, excursions and entertainment, partly in English (15/6-31/8). Exchange facilities. ATM. Safety deposit. Internet café. WiFi over site (charged). Dogs taken in one section. Torches required in some areas. Off site: Resort of L'Escala 5 km. Riding and boat launching 5 km. Water park 10 km. Golf 30 km.

Open: 18 May - 14 September.

Directions: L'Escala is northeast of Girona on coast between Palamós and Roses. From A7/E15 autostrada take exit 5 towards L'Escala on GI623. Turn north 2 km. before L'Escala towards Sant Marti d'Ampúrias. Site well signed.

GPS: 42.16098, 3.107774

Charges guide

Per unit incl. 2 persons and electricity	€ 22,50 - € 68,00
extra person	€ 3,50 - € 6,00
child (3-10 yrs)	€ 3,00 - € 3,50
dog	€ 3,20 - € 5,00

You might like to know

There is a special area with pitches for dog owners (dogs are not allowed in mobile homes or chalets).

- ☑ Dogs welcome *(subject to conditions)*
- ☑ Dogs welcome all season
- ○ Dogs welcome part season
- ○ Breed restrictions *(e.g. only small dogs accepted)*
- ☑ Number restrictions *(max. 1 or 2 dogs)*
- ☑ Dog sanitary facilities *(e.g. waste bins, bags)*
- ☑ Dog showers
- ☑ On-site dog walking area
- ○ Kennels
- ○ Vet nearby *(able to help with UK Pet Passports)*

Facilities:
Attractively tiled, fully equipped, large toilet blocks provide some cabins for each sex. Excellent facilities for disabled visitors, plus baths for children. One block has underfloor heating and family cabins with showers and basins. Laundry facilities. Gas supplies. Motorcaravan services. Full size refrigerators. Supermarket. Pleasant restaurant and bar with terrace. Takeaway. Purpose built play centre (with qualified attendant), playground and separate play area for toddlers. TV room. Surf Center. Fishing, sailing and boat launching. Minigolf. Bicycle hire. Barbecue and dance once weekly when numbers justify. ATM. Internet. WiFi over site (charged). Dogs are accepted in one section. (Note: no pool). Off site: Riding 6 km. Golf 15 km.

Open: 15 March - 2 November.

Directions: Attention: sat nav takes you on a different route, but easier to drive is from AP7 exit 3 (Figueres Nord) direction Roses on C-68. At roundabout Castello d'Empuries take second right to St Pere Pescador, cross town and river bridge. From there site is well signed.

GPS: 42.18092, 3.09425

Charges guide

Per person € 3,15 - € 4,35	
child (under 12 yrs) no charge - € 2,90	
pitch € 9,40 - € 46,90	
electricity € 3,80	

Discounts for pensioners on longer stays. No credit cards.

Camping Aquarius

Playa s/n, E-17470 Sant Pere Pescador (Girona)
t: 972 520 003   e: camping@aquarius.es
alanrogers.com/ES80500   www.aquarius.es

Accommodation: ☑ Pitch ☑ Mobile home/chalet ○ Hotel/B&B ○ Apartment

This is a welcoming and organised family site approached by an attractive road flanked by orchards. Aquarius has direct access to a quiet, sandy beach that slopes gently and provides good bathing. Watersports are popular, particularly windsurfing (a school is provided). One third of the site has good shade with a park-like atmosphere. There are 430 touring pitches, all with electricity (6/15A). Markus Rupp and his wife are keen to make every visitor's experience a happy one. The site is ideal for those who really like sun and sea, with a quiet situation. Mr Rupp has a background in architecture and a wealth of knowledge on the Catalan area and culture. He has written a booklet of suggested tours. The family is justifiably proud of their most attractive and absolutely pristine site which they continually upgrade and improve. The spotless beach bar complex with shaded terraces, satellite TV and evening entertainment, has marvellous views over the Bay of Roses. The Surf Center with rentals, school and shop is ideal for enthusiasts and beginners alike.

You might like to know

The site is located between fields and meadows and a long sandy. It is also close to several national parks, so exercising your dog should not be a problem. In low season dogs are free of charge.

- ☑ **Dogs welcome** *(subject to conditions)*
- ☑ **Dogs welcome all season**
- ○ **Dogs welcome part season**
- ○ **Breed restrictions** *(e.g. only small dogs accepted)*
- ○ **Number restrictions** *(max. 1 or 2 dogs)*
- ○ **Dog sanitary facilities** *(e.g. waste bins, bags)*
- ○ **Dog showers**
- ○ **On-site dog walking area**
- ○ **Kennels**
- ○ **Vet nearby** *(able to help with UK Pet Passports)*

Camping la Ballena Alegre

Ctra Sant Marti d'Empuries s/n, E-17470 Sant Pere Pescador (Girona)
t: 972 520 302 e: info@ballena-alegre.com
alanrogers.com/ES80600 www.ballena-alegre.com

Accommodation: ☑ Pitch ☑ Mobile home/chalet ○ Hotel/B&B ○ Apartment

La Ballena Alegre is a spacious site with almost 2 km. of frontage directly onto an excellent beach of soft golden sand (which is cleaned daily). They claim that none of the 966 touring pitches is more than 100 m. from the beach. The grass pitches are individually numbered, many separated by hedges, and there is a choice of size (up to 120 sq.m). Electrical connections (5/10A) are available in all areas and there are 670 fully serviced pitches. There are several bungalow areas within the site with their own small pools and play areas, and some have shared jacuzzis. This is a great site for families. There are restaurant and bar areas beside the pleasant terraced pool complex (four pools including a pool for children). For those who wish to drink and snack late there is a pub open until 03.00. The well managed, soundproofed disco is popular with youngsters. A little train ferries people along the length of the site and a road train runs to local villages. Plenty of entertainment and activities are offered, including a well managed watersports centre, with sub-aqua, windsurfing and kite-surfing, where equipment can be hired and lessons taken.

Facilities: Seven well maintained toilet blocks are of a very high standard. Facilities for children, babies and disabled visitors. Launderette. Motorcaravan services. Gas. Comprehensive range of restaurants, snack bars and takeaways, including a pizzeria/trattoria, arroceria, a pub, a self-service restaurant and a beach bar in high season. Swimming pool complex. Jacuzzi. Tennis. Watersports centre. Fitness centre. Bicycle hire. Playgrounds. Soundproofed disco. Dancing twice weekly and organised activities, sports, entertainment, etc. ATM. Dogs only allowed in one zone. Internet and WiFi (charged). Torches useful in beach areas. Off site: Go-karting nearby with bus service. Fishing 300 m. Riding 2 km.

Open: 17 May - 21 September.

Directions: From A7 Figueres-Girona autopista take exit 5 to L'Escala GI623 for 18.5 km. At roundabout take sign to Sant Marti d'Empúries and follow site signs.
GPS: 42.15323, 3.11248

Charges guide

Per unit incl. 2 persons and electricity	€ 26,50 - € 57,00
extra person	€ 4,00 - € 5,00
child (3-10 yrs)	€ 2,80 - € 3,30
dog	€ 2,30 - € 4,80

Discount of 10% on pitch charge for pensioners all season.
No credit cards.

You might like to know

In high season, a number of dog-friendly pitches are available (these are the only pitches which can be used for dogs).

- ☑ Dogs welcome *(subject to conditions)*
- ☑ Dogs welcome all season
- ○ Dogs welcome part season
- ○ Breed restrictions *(e.g. only small dogs accepted)*
- ☑ Number restrictions *(max. 1 or 2 dogs)*
- ○ Dog sanitary facilities *(e.g. waste bins, bags)*
- ○ Dog showers
- ○ On-site dog walking area
- ○ Kennels
- ○ Vet nearby *(able to help with UK Pet Passports)*

Facilities: One newly built and two mature sanitary blocks are well maintained. British style WCs, preset hot water in the showers. Toilet facilities for disabled campers. Facilities for babies. Washing machines and dryer. Motorcaravan services. Well stocked supermarket and roast chicken takeaway. Restaurant/bar. Fridge hire. Entertainment in high season. Gas. Bicycle hire. Communal barbecue. WiFi throughout (charged). Off site: Golf and riding 1.5 km. Oliva 3 km. with restaurants, cafés and supermarkets. Large street market on Fridays. Ideal area for cycling.

Open: All year.

Directions: From the north and AP7 exit 61 take N332 and drive through Oliva. From the south exit 62 and left for Oliva. Exit at km. 213 (south) or 210 (north) signed 'urbanisation'. At roundabout take fourth exit. Turn right before narrow bridge. Continue and bear right on Carrer de Xeraco. Site is on the left.

GPS: 38.905, -0.066

Charges guide

Per unit incl. 2 persons
and electricity € 24,02 - € 49,94

extra person € 3,96

child (2-10 yrs) € 2,77

dog € 2,00

Spain – Oliva

Euro Camping

Partida Rabdells s/n, CN332 km. 210, E-46780 Oliva (Valencia)
t: 962 854 098   e: info@eurocamping-es.com
alanrogers.com/ES86120   www.eurocamping-es.com

Accommodation: ⊘ Pitch ⊘ Mobile home/chalet ○ Hotel/B&B ○ Apartment

Approached through a new urbanisation, Euro Camping is a well maintained, British-owned site. Spacious and flat, it is set amidst many high trees, mainly eucalyptus, with its own access to a fine sandy beach. From reception, with its helpful English-speaking staff and interesting aviary opposite, wide tarmac or paved roads lead to 315 large, gravel-based pitches which are either marked or hedged (most are for touring units). The main site road leads down to a beachside restaurant with superb views and a supermarket.

You might like to know

There is direct access from the site onto a long sandy beach where, out of high season, dogs can swim in the Mediterranean.

- ⊘ Dogs welcome *(subject to conditions)*
- ⊘ Dogs welcome all season
- ○ Dogs welcome part season
- ○ Breed restrictions *(e.g. only small dogs accepted)*
- ⊘ Number restrictions *(max. 1 or 2 dogs)*
- ○ Dog sanitary facilities *(e.g. waste bins, bags)*
- ○ Dog showers
- ○ On-site dog walking area
- ○ Kennels
- ⊘ Vet nearby *(able to help with UK Pet Passports)*

Facilities: Nine clean toilet blocks of standard design, well spaced around the site, include washbasins (all with hot water). Laundry. Gas supplies. Large well stocked supermarket. Restaurant. Bar. Snack bar. Swimming pool complex (April-Sept). Indoor pool, gymnasium (April-Oct), sauna, jacuzzi and massage service. New outdoor fitness course for adults. Open-air family cinema (July/Aug). Tennis. Pétanque. Minigolf. Play area. Watersports school. Internet café (also WiFi). Winter activities including Spanish classes. Pet washing area.
Off site: Buses to Cartagena and Murcia from outside site. Golf, bicycle hire and riding 5 km.

Open: All year.

Directions: Use exit (Salida) 11 from MU312 dual carriageway towards Cabo de Palos, signed Playa Honda (site signed also). Cross road bridge and double back on yourself. Site entrance is clearly visible beside dual carriageway with many flags flying.
GPS: 37.62445, -0.74442

Charges guide

Per unit incl. 2 persons
and electricity € 20,00 - € 35,00

extra person € 4,10 - € 5,10

child (4-11 yrs) € 3,60 - € 4,10

dog € 1,25

Discounts and special prices for low season and long winter stays.

Caravaning La Manga

Autovia Cartagena-La Manga, Salida 11, E-30386 La Manga del Mar Menor (Murcia)
t: 968 563 014   e: lamanga@caravaning.es
alanrogers.com/ES87530   www.caravaning.es

Accommodation: ☑ Pitch   ☑ Mobile home/chalet   ○ Hotel/B&B   ○ Apartment

This is a very large, well equipped, holiday-style site with its own beach and both indoor and outdoor pools. With a good number of typical Spanish long stay units, the length of the site is impressive (1 km) and a bicycle is very helpful for getting about. The 1,000 regularly laid out, gravel touring pitches (100 or 110 sq.m) are generally separated by hedges which also provide a degree of shade. Each has a 10A electricity supply, water and the possibility of satellite TV reception. This site's excellent facilities are ideally suited for holidays in the winter when the weather is very pleasantly warm. Daytime temperatures in November usually exceed 20 degrees. If you are suffering from aches and pains try the famous local mud treatment. Reception will assist with bookings. La Manga is a 22 km. long, narrow strip of land, bordered by the Mediterranean on one side and by the Mar Menor on the other. The campsite is situated on the approach to 'the strip', enjoying the benefit of its own semi-private beach with impressive tall palm trees alongside the Mar Menor, which provides shallow warm waters, ideal for families with children.

You might like to know

Pets are not allowed in rented accommodation. The Regional Nature Reserve of Calblanque offers some good walking.

☑ Dogs welcome *(subject to conditions)*
☑ Dogs welcome all season
○ Dogs welcome part season
○ Breed restrictions *(e.g. only small dogs accepted)*
☑ Number restrictions *(max. 1 or 2 dogs)*
○ Dog sanitary facilities *(e.g. waste bins, bags)*
○ Dog showers
○ On-site dog walking area
○ Kennels
○ Vet nearby *(able to help with UK Pet Passports)*

Facilities: A newer toilet block, heated when necessary, has free hot showers but cold water to open plan washbasins. Facilities for disabled visitors. Small baby room. An older block in the original area has similar provision. Washing machine and dryer. Bar, restaurant, takeaway and supermarket (all 1/1-31/12). Outdoor swimming pool (1/4-31/10). Indoor pool (all year). Playground. Boules. Bicycle hire. Riding. Rafting. Only gas barbecues are permitted. Torches required in some areas. WiFi (free). Off site: Fishing 100 m. Skiing in season. Canoeing nearby.

Open: All year.

Directions: Site is 2 km. from Ainsa, on the road from Ainsa to France.
GPS: 42.4352, 0.13618

Charges guide

Per unit incl. 2 persons
and electricity € 25,25 - € 33,70

Spain – Labuerda

Camping Peña Montañesa

Ctra Ainsa-Francia km 2, E-22360 Labuerda (Huesca)
t: 974 500 032 e: info@penamontanesa.com
alanrogers.com/ES90600 www.penamontanesa.com

Accommodation: ☑ Pitch ☑ Mobile home/chalet ○ Hotel/B&B ○ Apartment

A large site situated quite high up in the Pyrenees near the Ordesa National Park, Peña Montañesa is easily accessible from Ainsa or from France via the Bielsa Tunnel (steep sections on the French side). The site is essentially divided into three sections opening progressively throughout the season and all have shade. The 288 pitches on fairly level grass are of about 75 sq.m. and 10A electricity is available on virtually all. Grouped near the entrance are the facilities that make the site so attractive, including a fair sized outdoor pool and a glass-covered indoor pool with jacuzzi and sauna. Here too is an attractive bar/restaurant with an open fire and a terrace; a supermarket and takeaway are opposite. There is an entertainment programme for children (21/6-15/9 and Easter weekend) and twice weekly for adults in July and August. This is quite a large site which has grown very quickly and as such, it may at times be a little hard pressed, although it is very well run. The site is ideally situated for exploring the beautiful Pyrenees. The complete town of Ainsa is listed as a national monument of Spain and should be explored while you are here.

You might like to know

The campsite is situated near the entrance of the Ordesa and Monte Perdido National Park. It is a comfortable site with easy access to dramatic Pyrenean countryside.

☑ **Dogs welcome** (subject to conditions)
☑ **Dogs welcome all season**
○ **Dogs welcome part season**
○ **Breed restrictions** (e.g. only small dogs accepted)
☑ **Number restrictions** (max. 1 or 2 dogs)
○ **Dog sanitary facilities** (e.g. waste bins, bags)
○ **Dog showers**
○ **On-site dog walking area**
○ **Kennels**
○ **Vet nearby** (able to help with UK Pet Passports)

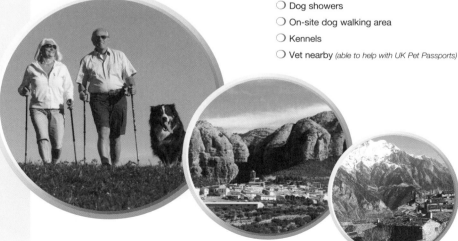

Facilities:
Facilities: The clean, well maintained toilet block is modern with British style toilets, open style washbasins and hot showers, plus beach showers. Facilities for disabled visitors and babies. Laundry facilities. Motorcaravan services. Supermarket, bar with satellite TV (1/6-30/9). Restaurant and takeaway (1/6-15/9). Bicycle hire. Entertainment in high season. Charcoal barbecues are permitted. Off site: Beach and fishing 100 m. Bus service 800 m. Kayak excursions. Birdwatching.

Open: All year.

Directions: From the north, turn off the main coast road (N13-E50) just after camping sign at end of embankment alongside estuary, 1.5 km. south of ferry. From the south on N13 turn left at Hotel Faz de Minho at start of estuary and follow for 1 km. through woods to site.

GPS: 41.86635, -8.85844

Charges guide

Per unit incl. 2 persons
and electricity € 15,00 - € 31,30

extra person € 3,40 - € 5,70

child (5-10 yrs) € 1,70 - € 2,90

dog € 1,00 - € 2,00

Off season discounts (up to 70%).

Orbitur Camping Caminha

EN13 km. 90, Mata do Camarido, P-4910-180 Caminha (Viana do Costelo)
t: 258 921 295   e: infocaminha@orbitur.pt
alanrogers.com/PO8010   www.orbitur.pt

Accommodation: ☑ Pitch ☑ Mobile home/chalet ○ Hotel/B&B ○ Apartment

In northern Portugal, close to the Spanish border, this pleasant site is just 200 m. from the beach. It has an attractive and peaceful setting in woods alongside the river estuary that marks the border with Spain and on the edge of the little town of Caminha. Of the 262 pitches, just 25 are available for touring with electricity (5/15A Europlug), the remainder are occupied by permanent units and chalets for rent. The site is shaded by tall pines with other small trees planted to mark large sandy pitches. The main site road is surfaced but elsewhere take care not to get trapped in soft sand. Pitching and parking can be haphazard. Static units are grouped together on one side of the site. Water points, electrical supply and lighting are good. With a pleasant, open feel about the setting, fishing and swimming are possible in the estuary, and from the rather open, sandy beach.

You might like to know

This site is just 200 m. from the beach, attractively situated in a pine forest on the Minho river estuary.

- ☑ Dogs welcome *(subject to conditions)*
- ☑ Dogs welcome all season
- ○ Dogs welcome part season
- ○ Breed restrictions *(e.g. only small dogs accepted)*
- ☑ Number restrictions *(max. 1 or 2 dogs)*
- ○ Dog sanitary facilities *(e.g. waste bins, bags)*
- ○ Dog showers
- ○ On-site dog walking area
- ○ Kennels
- ○ Vet nearby *(able to help with UK Pet Passports)*

Facilities
Facilities: The modern toilet blocks are clean, with 14 free hot showers and washing machines. Facilities for disabled visitors. Motorcaravan services. Gas supplies. Shop. Bar. Restaurant and takeaway (1/6-15/9). TV room. Play area. Bicycle hire. Free WiFi at the bar. Bungalows (7) to rent. Off site: Bus service 150 m. (summer only). Fishing and beach 200 m. Indoor pool, lake swimming and riding at Mira 7 km.

Open: 23 March - 30 September.

Directions: Take the IP5 (A25) southwest to Aveiro then the A17 south to Figuera da Foz. Then take the N109 north to Mira and follow signs west to Praia (beach) de Mira.

GPS: 40.4533, -8.79902

Charges guide

Per person € 5,80	
child (5-10 yrs) € 2,90	
pitch € 8,60 - € 11,90	
electricity € 3,50 - € 4,60	

Off season discounts (up to 70%).

Portugal – Praia de Mira

Orbitur Camping Mira

Estrada Florestal no 1 km. 2, Dunas de Mira, P-3070-792 Praia de Mira (Coimbra)
t: 231 471 234 e: infomira@orbitur.pt
alanrogers.com/PO8070 www.orbitur.pt

Accommodation: ⦿ Pitch ⦿ Mobile home/chalet ○ Hotel/B&B ○ Apartment

A small, peaceful seaside site set in pinewoods, Orbitur Camping Mira is situated to the south of Aveiro and Vagos, in a quieter and less crowded area. It fronts onto a lake at the head of the Ria de Mira, which eventually runs into the Aveiro Ria. A back gate leads directly to the sea and a wide quiet beach 300 m. away. A road runs alongside the site boundary where the restaurant complex is situated resulting in some road noise. The site has around 225 pitches on sand, which are not marked but have trees creating natural divisions. Electricity and water points are plentiful. The site provides an inexpensive restaurant, snack bar, lounge bar and TV lounge. A medium sized supermarket is well stocked, with plenty of fresh produce. The Mira Ria is fascinating, with the brightly painted, decorative 'moliceiros' (traditional fishing boats).

You might like to know

A gate at the back of the campsite opens directly onto a wide sandy beach.

- ☑ Dogs welcome *(subject to conditions)*
- ☑ Dogs welcome all season
- ○ Dogs welcome part season
- ○ Breed restrictions *(e.g. only small dogs accepted)*
- ☑ Number restrictions *(max. 1 or 2 dogs)*
- ○ Dog sanitary facilities *(e.g. waste bins, bags)*
- ○ Dog showers
- ○ On-site dog walking area
- ○ Kennels
- ○ Vet nearby *(able to help with UK Pet Passports)*

Facilities: Eight toilet blocks provide comprehensive facilities, including those for children and disabled visitors. Bar. Restaurant. Crêperie. Takeaway. Large supermarket. Swimming pool. Covered pool. Wellness centre. Sports field. Games room. Play area, farm and play house. Tennis. Bicycle hire. Activity and entertainment programme. Mobile homes and caravans for rent. Caravan repair and servicing. The site's own debit card system is used for payment at all facilities. Off site: Vicentina coast and the Alentejo Natural Park. Sines (birthplace of Vasco de Gama). Cycle and walking tracks. Sea fishing.

Open: All year.

Directions: From the N120 from Odemira to Lagos, at roundabout in the centre of Portas de Transval turn towards Milfontes. Take turn to Cabo Sardâo and then Zambujeira do Mar. Site is on the left.

GPS: 37.60422, -8.73142

Charges guide

Per unit incl. up to 4 persons
and electricity € 20,00 - € 50,00

extra person € 5,00 - € 10,00

child (4-12 yrs) € 5,00

Zmar-Eco Camping Resort

Herdade A de Mateus EN393/1, San Salvador, P-7630 Odemira (Beja)
t: 707 200 626 e: info@zmar.eu
alanrogers.com/PO8175 www.zmar.eu

Accommodation: ☑ Pitch ☑ Mobile home/chalet ○ Hotel/B&B ○ Apartment

Zmar is an exciting new project which should be fully open this year. The site is located near Zambujeira do Mar, on the Alentejo coast. This is a highly ambitious initiative developed along very strict environmental lines. For example, renewable resources such as locally harvested timber and recycled plastic are used wherever possible and solar energy is used whenever practicable. Public indoor spaces have no air conditioning, but there is adequate cooling through underfloor ventilation and electric fans where possible. Pitches are 100 sq.m. and benefit from artificial shade. Caravans and wood-clad mobile homes are also available for rent. The swimming pool complex features a large outdoor pool and an indoor pool area with a wave machine and a wellness centre. The very large and innovative children's play park has climbing nets, labyrinths and caves. There is also a children's farm and a large play house. For adults, many sporting amenities will be available around the resort's 81 hectare park. Zmar's self-service restaurant will open throughout the season.

You might like to know

Zmar-Eco Camping Resort & Spa was developed according to strict environmental criteria, primarily using renewable resources such as locally-sourced wood and stone.

- ☑ Dogs welcome *(subject to conditions)*
- ☑ Dogs welcome all season
- ○ Dogs welcome part season
- ○ Breed restrictions *(e.g. only small dogs accepted)*
- ○ Number restrictions *(max. 1 or 2 dogs)*
- ○ Dog sanitary facilities *(e.g. waste bins, bags)*
- ○ Dog showers
- ○ On-site dog walking area
- ○ Kennels
- ○ Vet nearby *(able to help with UK Pet Passports)*

Facilities: Four toilet blocks are well located around the site. Two have been refurbished, two are new and contain modern facilities for disabled campers. Hot water throughout. Facilities for children. Dog shower. Washing machines. Shop. Gas supplies. Restaurant/bar. Swimming pool (Mar-Oct) with two terraces and new jacuzzi. Aqua gymnastics. New wellness facility (2012). Bicycle hire. Entertainment in high season on the bar terrace. Two children's playgrounds. Adult art workshops. Miniclub (5-12 yrs) in season. Boules. Archery. Sports field. Cable TV. Internet. WiFi on payment. Bungalows to rent. Off site: Bus to Lagos and other towns from Praia da Luz village 1.5 km. Fishing and beach 2 km. Golf 3 km. Sailing and boat launching 5 km. Riding 7 km.

Open: All year.

Directions: Take exit 1 from the N125 Lagos-Vila do Bispo. The impressive entrance is 3 km. on the right.

GPS: 37.10111, -8.73278

Charges guide

Per unit incl. 2 persons and electricity € 17,00 - € 33,00	
extra person € 4,00 - € 6,50	
child (3-10 yrs) no charge - € 3,50	
dog € 5,00	

Portugal – Lagos

Yelloh! Village Turiscampo

EN125, Espiche, Luz, P-8600 Lagos (Faro)
t: **282 789 265** e: info@turiscampo.com
alanrogers.com/PO8202 www.yellohvillage.co.uk/camping/turiscampo

Accommodation: ☑ Pitch ☑ Mobile home/chalet ○ Hotel/B&B ○ Apartment

This good quality site has been thoughtfully refurbished and updated since it was purchased by the friendly Coll family, who are known to us from their previous Spanish site. The site provides 206 pitches (70 sq.m) for touring units, mainly in rows of terraces, all with electricity (6/10A) and some with shade. Thirty-six deluxe pitches have water and waste water. The upper areas of the site are mainly used for bungalow accommodation (and are generally separate from the touring areas). A new, elevated, Californian-style pool and a children's pool have been constructed. The supporting structure is a clever water cascade and surround, with a large sun lounger area on astroturf. One side of the pool area is open to the road. The restaurant/bar has been tastefully refurbished and Roberto and his staff are delighted to use their excellent English, providing good fare at most reasonable prices. The restaurant has two patios, one of which is used for live entertainment and discos in season, and the other for dining out. The sea is 2 km. away and the city of Lagos 4 km. with all the attractions of the Algarve within easy reach.

You might like to know

Lagos was capital of the kingdom of the Algarve from the 16th to the 18th centuries and remains a great seafaring port.

- ☑ Dogs welcome *(subject to conditions)*
- ☑ Dogs welcome all season
- ○ Dogs welcome part season
- ○ Breed restrictions *(e.g. only small dogs accepted)*
- ☑ Number restrictions *(max. 1 or 2 dogs)*
- ○ Dog sanitary facilities *(e.g. waste bins, bags)*
- ○ Dog showers
- ○ On-site dog walking area
- ○ Kennels
- ○ Vet nearby *(able to help with UK Pet Passports)*

Facilities: Three spacious toilet blocks are showing some signs of wear but provide hot and cold showers and washbasins with cold water. Washing machines. Motorcaravan services. Supermarket (July/Aug). Bar (June-Sept). Restaurant (July/Aug). TV room. Satellite TV in restaurant. Bicycle hire. Barbecue area. Playground. Fishing. Medical post. Car wash. Free WiFi over part of site. Off site: Buses from village 1 km. Beach and fishing 2.5 km. Boat launching 8 km. Golf 12 km.

Open: All year.

Directions: From Sagres, turn off N268 road west onto the EN268. After 2 km. the site is signed off to the right.

GPS: 37.02278, -8.94583

Charges guide

Per person € 5,80	
child (5-10 yrs) € 2,90	
caravan and car € 8,00 - € 10,10	
electricity (6A) € 3,50 - € 4,60	

Off season discounts (up to 70%).

Orbitur Camping Sagres

Cerro das Moitas, P-8650-998 Sagres (Faro)
t: 282 624 371   e: infosagres@orbitur.pt
alanrogers.com/PO8430   www.orbitur.pt

Accommodation: ☑ Pitch ☑ Mobile home/chalet ○ Hotel/B&B ○ Apartment

Camping Sagres is a pleasant site at the western tip of the Algarve, not very far from a lighthouse in the relatively unspoilt southwest corner of Portugal. With 960 pitches for tents and 120 for tourers, the sandy pitches, some terraced, are located amongst pine trees that give good shade. There are some hardstandings for motorcaravans and electricity throughout. The fairly bland restaurant, bar and café/grill provide a range of reasonably priced meals. This is a reasonable site for those seeking winter sun, or as a base for exploring this 'Land's End' region of Portugal. It is away from the hustle and bustle of the more crowded resorts. The beaches and the town of Sagres (the departure point of the Portuguese navigators) with its fort, are a short drive.

You might like to know

The first Portuguese caravelas to discover the New World set sail from Sagres.

☑ Dogs welcome *(subject to conditions)*
☑ Dogs welcome all season
○ Dogs welcome part season
○ Breed restrictions *(e.g. only small dogs accepted)*
☑ Number restrictions *(max. 1 or 2 dogs)*
○ Dog sanitary facilities *(e.g. waste bins, bags)*
○ Dog showers
○ On-site dog walking area
○ Kennels
○ Vet nearby *(able to help with UK Pet Passports)*

Facilities:
Three superb toilet blocks are kept pristine and have hot water throughout. Facilities for disabled visitors. Washing machines. Large supermarket and shopping centre, bars, restaurants, cafés and pizzeria (all season; takeaway service 15/5-30/9). Excellent pool complex with slide and spa centre (30/3-25/9). Tennis. Games room. Playground. Children's clubs. Entertainment programme. WiFi (charged). Direct beach access. Windsurf and pedalo hire. Mobile homes, chalets and 14 eco apartments for rent. Off site: ATM 500 m. Riding and boat launching 1 km. Golf and fishing 4 km. Walking and cycling trails. Excursions to Venice.

Open: 28 March - 30 September.

Directions: From A4 autostrada (approaching from Milan) take Mestre exit and follow signs initially for Venice airport and then Jesolo. From Jesolo, follow signs to Cavallino from where site is well signed.

GPS: 45.47380, 12.54903

Charges guide

Per unit incl. 2 persons and electricity € 20,00 - € 50,40
extra person € 5,00 - € 10,90
child (2-5 yrs) € 3,35 - € 9,90
dog € 2,65 - € 5,90

Camping Village Europa

Via Fausta 332, I-30013 Cavallino-Treporti (Veneto)
t: 041 968 069   e: info@campingeuropa.com
alanrogers.com/IT60410   www.campingeuropa.com

Accommodation: ☑ Pitch   ☑ Mobile home/chalet   ○ Hotel/B&B   ☑ Apartment

Europa is a large site in a great position with direct access to a fine, sandy, Blue Flag beach with lifeguards. There are 500 touring pitches, 450 of which have 8A electricity, water, drainage and satellite TV connections. There is a separate area for campers with dogs, and some smaller pitches are available for those with tents. The site is kept beautifully clean and neat and there is an impressive array of restaurants, bars, shops and leisure amenities. These are cleverly laid out along an avenue and include a jeweller's, a doctor's surgery, Internet services and much more. Leisure facilities are arranged around the site. The touring area is surprisingly peaceful for a site of this size. A professional team provides entertainment and regular themed summer events. Some restaurant tables have pleasant sea views. Venice is easily accessible by bus and then ferry from Punta Sabbioni.

You might like to know

The Cavallino coast is a peaceful and green peninsula facing north towards the open sea, and south towards the Venetian lagoon.

- ☑ Dogs welcome *(subject to conditions)*
- ☑ Dogs welcome all season
- ○ Dogs welcome part season
- ○ Breed restrictions *(e.g. only small dogs accepted)*
- ☑ Number restrictions *(max. 1 or 2 dogs)*
- ☑ Dog sanitary facilities *(e.g. waste bins, bags)*
- ☑ Dog showers
- ○ On-site dog walking area
- ○ Kennels
- ○ Vet nearby *(able to help with UK Pet Passports)*

Facilities

Facilities: Nine modern toilet blocks are maintained to a high standard with good hot showers and a reasonable proportion of British style toilets. Good provision for disabled visitors. Washing machines and dryers. Range of shops. Several bars, restaurants and takeaways. Swimming pool complex with slides and flumes. Several play areas. Tennis. Surfboard and catamaran hire. Wide range of organised entertainment. WiFi in the Bar Blu and Bar Rosa, Piazza Europa and the telephone office. Church. Special area and facilities for dog owners (also beach area). Off site: Fishing 1 km. Riding 7 km. Golf 10 km.

Open: 12 April - 30 September.

Directions: From A4 motorway, take Jesolo exit. After Jesolo continue towards Punta Sabbioni. Site is clearly signed to the left towards the end of this road, close to the Venice ferries.

GPS: 45.43750, 12.43805

Charges guide

Per unit incl. 2 persons and electricity	€ 21,40 - € 47,70
extra person	€ 4,60 - € 10,50
child or senior (2-5 and over 60)	€ 3,80 - € 8,50
dog	€ 1,30 - € 4,20

Italy – Punta Sabbioni

Camping Marina di Venezia

Via Montello 6, I-30013 Punta Sabbioni (Veneto)
t: 041 530 2511   e: camping@marinadivenezia.it
alanrogers.com/IT60450   www.marinadivenezia.it

Accommodation: ☑ Pitch   ☑ Mobile home/chalet   ○ Hotel/B&B   ○ Apartment

This is a very large site (2,915 pitches) with much the same atmosphere as many other large sites along this appealing stretch of coastline. Marina di Venezia, however, has the advantage of being within walking distance of the ferry to Venice. It will appeal in particular to those who enjoy an extensive range of entertainment and activities and a lively atmosphere. Individual pitches are marked out on sandy or grassy ground; most are separated by trees or hedges. They are of average size for the region (around 80 sq.m) and all are equipped with electricity and water. The site's excellent sandy beach is one of the widest along this stretch of coast and has five pleasant beach bars. The 15,000 sq.m. wide, multi-level AquaMarina Park has exceptional facilities – a feature pool for children with slides and a cascade, an Olympic size pool with massage jets, a lagoon with disability access, and a wave pool with a beach. There are charming features for the youngest campers, a choice of whirlpool and a solarium on grass, plus an impressive 45-metre panoramic bridge. This is a well run site with committed management and staff.

You might like to know

Dogs are not permitted on the beach and must always be kept on a lead at the campsite.

- ☑ Dogs welcome *(subject to conditions)*
- ☑ Dogs welcome all season
- ○ Dogs welcome part season
- ○ Breed restrictions *(e.g. only small dogs accepted)*
- ○ Number restrictions *(max. 1 or 2 dogs)*
- ☑ Dog sanitary facilities *(e.g. waste bins, bags)*
- ☑ Dog showers
- ☑ On-site dog walking area
- ○ Kennels
- ☑ Vet nearby *(able to help with UK Pet Passports)*

Camping Val Rendena

Via Civico 117, I-38080 Darè (Trentino - Alto Adige)
t: 046 580 1669 e: info@campingvalrendena.com
alanrogers.com/IT62135 www.campingvalrendena.com

Accommodation: ☑ Pitch ☑ Mobile home/chalet ○ Hotel/B&B ○ Apartment

Facilities: Two sanitary units, a small one in the reception block, a larger one at centre of site have hot water, controllable showers and washbasins in cabins. Facilities for disabled visitors. Baby room. Laundry. Motorcaravan service area. Shop selling essentials. Solar heated swimming pool with adjoining children's pool (1/6-30/9). Large playing field. Play area and play room. Bicycle hire. Communal barbecue. Massage and other treatments by appointment. Eight apartments to rent. Off site: Pizza restaurant adjoins site. Thermal baths. Golf. Tennis.

Open: 10 May - 30 September.

Directions: Site is 35 km. northwest of Trento. From A22 (E45) Brenner - Verona autostrada take exit for Trento-Centro. Then travel westerly on SS45b to Sarche, then SS237 to Ponte Arche and Tione di Trento. From here head north on SS239 towards Madonna di Campiglio for 10 km. to Darè. Immediately after entering Darè take descending slip road to right then follow camping signs to site beside river. Do not follow GPS instructions to enter a small lane to the right before Darè as this leads to a very narrow, height-restricted bridge.

GPS: 46.07440, 10.71718

Charges guide

Per unit incl. 2 persons
and electricity € 24,60 - € 28,60

extra person € 7,80 - € 8,80

child (3-12 yrs) € 6,80 - € 7,80

dog € 3,00 - € 3,50

Set in the Adamello Brenta National Park, a refuge of the European brown bear, Camping Val Rendena, is an enthusiastically run family site with a very friendly feel. There are 52 level grass touring pitches with some tree shade, all with 6A electricity and spread out between the seasonal pitches. The site's location makes it an ideal base from which to explore this beautiful region, rich in flora and fauna, where wooded hills with many marked paths reach up to 1,800 m. Beside the site runs the Sarca river, bordered for much of its journey by a cycleway. The park has several interesting information centres, including one at Spormaggiore, where brown bears can be observed. In the friendly reception a host of very useful park information is available, informing visitors of what this region has to offer. At the top of the valley is the 1,500 m. high ski resort of Madonna di Campiglio where, below the tree line, forests of larch and pine shade the endless routes for walkers, mountain bike and cycle riders. A bus service is provided by the site to a ski centre just 5 km. away.

You might like to know

A dog sitting service is offered, and there is a vet 5 km. away.

- ☑ Dogs welcome *(subject to conditions)*
- ☑ Dogs welcome all season
- ○ Dogs welcome part season
- ○ Breed restrictions *(e.g. only small dogs accepted)*
- ☑ Number restrictions *(max. 1 or 2 dogs)*
- ○ Dog sanitary facilities *(e.g. waste bins, bags)*
- ○ Dog showers
- ☑ On-site dog walking area
- ☑ Kennels
- ☑ Vet nearby *(able to help with UK Pet Passports)*

Camping Lago di Levico

Localitá Pleina, I-38056 Levico Terme (Trentino - Alto Adige)
t: 046 170 6491 e: info@campinglevico.com
alanrogers.com/IT62290 www.campinglevico.com

Accommodation: ☑ Pitch ☑ Mobile home/chalet ○ Hotel/B&B ○ Apartment

Camping Lago di Levico, by a pretty lakeside in the mountains, is the merger of two popular sites, Camping Levico and Camping Jolly. Brothers Andrea and Geno Antoniolli are making great improvements; already, there is an impressive new reception and further developments of the lakeside and swimming areas are planned. The lakeside pitches are quite special. There are 430 mostly grassy and shaded pitches (70-120 sq.m) with 6A electricity, 150 also have water and drainage and 12 have private facilities. Staff are welcoming and fluent in English. The swimming pool complex is popular, as is the summer family entertainment. There is a small supermarket on site and it is a short distance to the local village. The restaurant, bar, pizzeria and takeaway are open all season. The beautiful grass shores of the lake are ideal for sunbathing and the crystal clear water is ideal for enjoying (non-motorised) water activities. This is a site where the natural beauty of an Italian lake can be enjoyed without being overwhelmed by commercial tourism.

Facilities: Four modern sanitary blocks provide hot water for showers, washbasins and washing. Mostly British style toilets. Single locked unit for disabled visitors. Laundry facilities. Freezer. Motorcaravan service point. Good shop. Bar/restaurant and takeaway. Outdoor swimming pool. Play area. Miniclub and entertainment (high season). Fishing. Satellite TV and cartoon cinema. Internet access (free in low season). Kayak hire. Tennis. Torches useful. Bicycle hire. Off site: Boat launching 500 m. Bicycle track 1.5 km. Town with all the usual facilities and ATM 2 km. Riding 3 km. Golf 7 km.

Open: 20 March - 15 October.

Directions: From A22 Verona-Bolzano road take turn for Trento on S47 to Levico Terme where campsite is very well signed.

GPS: 46.00799, 11.28454

Charges guide

Per unit incl. 2 persons and electricity	€ 9,50 - € 38,00
extra person	€ 3,00 - € 14,25
child (3-11 yrs)	no charge - € 6,50
dog	no charge - € 5,00

You might like to know

There is a large private beach. The clean, shallow waters of the lake offer opportunities for swimming, fishing, canoeing and boating. Canoes and pedalos can be hired from reception.

- ☑ Dogs welcome *(subject to conditions)*
- ☑ Dogs welcome all season
- ○ Dogs welcome part season
- ○ Breed restrictions *(e.g. only small dogs accepted)*
- ☑ Number restrictions *(max. 1 or 2 dogs)*
- ☑ Dog sanitary facilities *(e.g. waste bins, bags)*
- ○ Dog showers
- ☑ On-site dog walking area
- ○ Kennels
- ○ Vet nearby *(able to help with UK Pet Passports)*

Tiliguerta Camping Village

S.P. 97 km. 6 - Loc. Capo Ferrato, I-09043 Muravera (Sardinia)
t: 070 991 437 e: info@tiliguerta.com
alanrogers.com/IT69750 www.tiliguerta.com

Accommodation: ☑ Pitch ☑ Mobile home/chalet ☑ Hotel/B&B ○ Apartment

Facilities: Three sanitary blocks. One is newly renovated with private bathrooms, and facilities for children and disabled visitors. The two older blocks have mixed Turkish/British style toilets. Washing machine. Motorcaravan service point (extra charge). Shop. Restaurant and snack bar. Play areas (due for replacement). Miniclub and entertainment in high season. Tennis. Water aerobics. Sub-aqua diving. Windsurfing school. Riding. Torches essential. Bicycle hire. WiFi over site (charged). Communal barbecue areas. Off site: Sailing 1.5 km.

Open: 27 April - 27 October.

Directions: Site is in southeast corner of Sardinia in the north of the Costa Rei. From coast road SS125 or the SP97 at km. 6, take the turn to Villaggio Capo Ferrato. Site is well signed from here.

GPS: 39.2923, 9.5987

Charges guide

Per unit incl. 2 persons and electricity	€ 21,50 - € 47,54
extra person	€ 5,00 - € 15,00
child (3-9 yrs)	€ 3,50 - € 10,00
dog	€ 3,00 - € 6,00

This family site situated at Capo Ferrato has changed its owners, name and direction (2011). The new owners have made many improvements, all of them in sympathy with the environment. The 186 reasonably sized pitches are on sand and have 3A electricity. Some have shade and views of the superb, fine beach and sea beyond. There are some permanent pitches used by Italian units. The traditional site buildings are centrally located and contain a good quality restaurant using only fresh ingredients. This has a charming ambience with its high arched ceilings. Shaded terraces allow comfortable viewing of the ambitious entertainment programme. Cars must be parked away from pitches. The staff are cheerful and English is spoken. Consideration is given to the environment at every turn. There are numerous activities on offer – basketball, beach volleyball, riding and watersports, and in high season, yoga, tai-chi, pilates and dancing. There is a full entertainment programme. We believe Tiliguerta is becoming a good quality, environmentally friendly site.

You might like to know

Tilguerta's dog friendly beach is rather special – stretching for over 500 sq.m. with a wealth of amenities including bowls of fresh water always available, a dog sitter, snack foods for dogs and much more.

- ☑ Dogs welcome *(subject to conditions)*
- ☑ Dogs welcome all season
- ○ Dogs welcome part season
- ○ Breed restrictions *(e.g. only small dogs accepted)*
- ○ Number restrictions *(max. 1 or 2 dogs)*
- ☑ Dog sanitary facilities *(e.g. waste bins, bags)*
- ☑ Dog showers
- ☑ On-site dog walking area
- ☑ Kennels
- ☑ Vet nearby *(able to help with UK Pet Passports)*

Camping Polari

Polari bb, HR-52210 Rovinj (Istria)
t: 052 801 501 e: polari@maistra.hr
alanrogers.com/CR6732 www.CampingRovinjVrsar.com

Accommodation: ◉ Pitch ◉ Mobile home/chalet ○ Hotel/B&B ○ Apartment

This 60-hectare site has excellent facilities for both textile and naturist campers, the latter in an area of 12 hectares to the left of the main site. There is shade here from a good covering of trees. In all, the site has 1,650 pitches for touring units which are level with some shade. All have access to 10A electricity. There is something for everyone to enjoy here or you might prefer to just relax in this quiet location. An impressive swimming pool complex is child friendly with large paddling areas. The ancient town of Rovinj is well worth a visit, although parking is difficult. It is best reached via the 4.5 km. coastal cycle path or by bus from the campsite. Part of the Maistra group, a massive improvement programme has been undertaken and the result makes it a very attractive option. Enjoy a meal on the huge restaurant terrace with panoramic views of the sea.

You might like to know

The campsite is surrounded and shaded by evergreen trees, a perfect area for exercising your dog.

- ◉ Dogs welcome *(subject to conditions)*
- ◉ Dogs welcome all season
- ○ Dogs welcome part season
- ○ Breed restrictions *(e.g. only small dogs accepted)*
- ○ Number restrictions *(max. 1 or 2 dogs)*
- ○ Dog sanitary facilities *(e.g. waste bins, bags)*
- ◉ Dog showers
- ◉ On-site dog walking area
- ○ Kennels
- ○ Vet nearby *(able to help with UK Pet Passports)*

Facilities: All the sanitary facilities have been renovated to a high standard with plenty of hot water and good showers. Washing machines and dryers. Laundry service including ironing. Motorcaravan service point. Two shops, one large and one small, one restaurant and snack bar. Tennis. Minigolf. Children's entertainment with all major European languages spoken. Bicycle hire. Watersports. Sailing school. Off site: Riding 1 km. Five buses daily to and from Rovinj 3 km. Golf 30 km.

Open: 1 April - 2 October.

Directions: From any access road to Rovinj look for red signs to AC Polari (amongst other destinations). The site is 3 km. south of Rovinj.

GPS: 45.06286, 13.67489

Charges guide

Per unit incl. 2 persons
and electricity € 18,00 - € 36,10

extra person (18-64 yrs)	€ 5,00 - € 9,30
child (5-17 yrs)	€ 4,00 - € 7,50
dog	€ 3,10 - € 6,50

For stays less than 3 nights in high season add 20%.

Arenaturist Camping Stoja

Stoja 37, HR-52100 Pula (Istria)
t: 052 387 144   e: acstoja@arenaturist.hr
alanrogers.com/CR6742   www.arenacamps.com

Accommodation: ☑ Pitch   ☑ Mobile home/chalet   ○ Hotel/B&B   ○ Apartment

Camping Stoja in Pula is an attractive and well maintained site on a small peninsula and therefore almost completely surrounded by the waters of the clear Adriatic. In the centre of the site is the old Fort Stoja, built in 1884 for coastal defence. Some of its buildings are now used as a toilet block and laundry and its courtyard is used by the entertainment team. The 708 touring pitches here vary greatly in size (50-120 sq.m) and are marked by round, concrete, numbered blocks, separated by young trees. About half have shade from mature trees and all are slightly sloping on grass and gravel. Pitches close to the pebble and rock beach have beautiful views of the sea and Pula. This site is an ideal base for visiting Pula, considered to be the capital of Istrian tourism and full of history, tradition and natural beauty, including a spectacular Roman amphitheatre.

You might like to know

This site is in an idyllic setting surrounded by rich pine forests and Mediterranean plants, with beaches that slope gently into the sea.

☑ Dogs welcome *(subject to conditions)*
☑ Dogs welcome all season
○ Dogs welcome part season
○ Breed restrictions *(e.g. only small dogs accepted)*
☑ Number restrictions *(max. 1 or 2 dogs)*
○ Dog sanitary facilities *(e.g. waste bins, bags)*
○ Dog showers
○ On-site dog walking area
○ Kennels
○ Vet nearby *(able to help with UK Pet Passports)*

Facilities: Five toilet blocks with British and Turkish style toilets, open plan washbasins with cold water only and controllable hot showers. Child size basins. Facilities for disabled visitors. Laundry and ironing service. Fridge box hire. Motorcaravan service point. Supermarket. Bar/restaurant. Miniclub and teen club. Bicycle hire. Water skiing. Boat hire. Boat launching. Surfboard and pedalo hire. Fishing (with permit). Island excursions. WiFi. Off site: Pula (walking distance). Riding 8 km. Golf 10 km.

Open: 30 March - 4 November.

Directions: From Pula follow site signs.
GPS: 44.85972, 13.81450

Charges guide

Per unit incl. 2 persons and electricity	€ 19,00 - € 32,10
extra person	€ 5,00 - € 7,80
child (4-12 yrs)	€ 2,50 - € 5,00
dog	€ 3,00 - € 4,80

Camping Kovacine

Melin I/20, HR-51557 Cres (Kvarner)
t: 051 573 150 e: campkovacine@kovacine.com
alanrogers.com/CR6765 www.camp-kovacine.com

Accommodation: ☑ Pitch ☑ Mobile home/chalet ○ Hotel/B&B ○ Apartment

Camping Kovacine is located on a peninsula on the beautiful Kvarner island of Cres, just 2 km. from the town of the same name. The site has 1002 numbered, mostly level pitches, of which 952 are for tourers (300 with 12A electricity). On sloping ground, partially shaded by mature olive and pine trees, pitching is on the large, open spaces between the trees. Some places have views of the Valun lagoon. Kovacine is partly an FKK (naturist) site, which is quite common in Croatia, and has a pleasant atmosphere. Here one can enjoy local live music on a stage close to the pebble beach (Blue Flag), where there is also a restaurant and bar. The site has its own beach, part concrete, part pebbles, and a jetty for mooring boats and fishing. It is close to the historic town of Cres, the main town on the island, which offers a rich history of fishing, shipyards and authentic Kvarner-style houses. There are also several bars, restaurants and shops.

You might like to know

Pets stay free of charge in low season.

- ☑ Dogs welcome *(subject to conditions)*
- ☑ Dogs welcome all season
- ○ Dogs welcome part season
- ☑ Breed restrictions *(e.g. only small dogs accepted)*
- ☑ Number restrictions *(max. 1 or 2 dogs)*
- ○ Dog sanitary facilities *(e.g. waste bins, bags)*
- ○ Dog showers
- ○ On-site dog walking area
- ○ Kennels
- ○ Vet nearby *(able to help with UK Pet Passports)*

Facilities: Modern, comfortable toilet blocks (two refurbished) offer British style toilets, equipped with solar power, open plan washbasins (some cabins for ladies) and hot showers. Private family bathroom for hire. Facilities for disabled visitors plus facilities for children. Laundry sinks and washing machine. Fridge box hire. Motorcaravan service point. Car wash. Mini-marina and boat crane. Supermarket, bar (Easter-19/10). Restaurant and pizzeria (May-15/10). Playground. Daily children's club. Evening shows with live music. Boat launching. Fishing. Diving centre. Motorboat hire. WiFi (free). Airport transfers. Off site: Wellness and fitness centre 0.5 km. Historic town of Cres with bars, restaurants and shops 2 km.

Open: 11 April - 19 October.

Directions: From Rijeka take no. 2 road south towards Labin and take ferry to Cres at Brestova. Continue to Cres and follow site signs.
GPS: 44.96188, 14.39650

Charges guide

Per unit incl. 2 persons and electricity	€ 17,80 - € 36,20
extra person	€ 6,00 - € 12,20
child (3-12 yrs)	€ 2,80 - € 5,00
dog	no charge - € 3,00

Facilities: Four new and two refurbished toilet blocks provide toilets, open style washbasins and controllable hot showers. Facilities for children and for disabled visitors. Laundry with sinks and washing machine. Fridge box hire. Car wash. Shop. Bar, restaurant, grill restaurant, pizzeria and fish restaurant. Playground. Minigolf. Fishing. Bicycle hire. Diving centre. Pedalo, canoe and boat hire. Excursions to the Blue Cave. WiFi (charged). Only gas and electric barbecues permitted. Off site: Boat launching 1 km. Martinscica with bars, restaurants and shops 2 km.

Open: 23 March - 1 October.

Directions: From Rijeka take no. 2 road south towards Labin and take ferry to Cres at Brestova. From Cres go south towards Martinscica and follow site signs.

GPS: 44.82333, 14.34083

Charges guide

Per unit incl. 2 persons and electricity	€ 15,00 - € 22,00
extra person	€ 5,00 - € 8,00
child (7-12 yrs)	€ 3,00 - € 5,00
dog	€ 3,50

Croatia – Martinscica

Camping Slatina

Martinscica, HR-51556 Cres (Kvarner)
t: 051 574 127   e: info@camp-slatina.com
alanrogers.com/CR6768   www.camps-cres-losinj.com

Accommodation: ☑ Pitch   ☑ Mobile home/chalet   ○ Hotel/B&B   ○ Apartment

Camping Slatina lies about halfway along the island of Cres, beside the fishing port of Martinscica, on a bay of the Adriatic Sea. It has 370 pitches for touring units, many with 10A electricity, 50 new individual ones (29 fully serviced) off very steep, tarmac access roads, sloping down to the sea. The pitches are large and level on a gravel base and enjoy plenty of shade from mature laurel trees, although hardly any have views. Whilst there is plenty of privacy, the site does have an enclosed feeling. Some pitches in the lower areas have water, electricity and drainage. Like so many sites in Croatia, Slatina has a private diving centre. Cres is surrounded by reefs and little islands and the crystal clear waters of the Adriatic make it perfect for diving. Martinscica owes its name to the medieval church of the Holy Martin and has a Glagolite monastery, standing next to the 17th-century castle, built by the Patrician Sforza. Both are well worth a visit.

You might like to know

Slatina's innovative project 'Camping cum cane' makes this an ideal site for dogs and their owners, but is still a great site for those without pets.

- ☑ Dogs welcome *(subject to conditions)*
- ☑ Dogs welcome all season
- ○ Dogs welcome part season
- ○ Breed restrictions *(e.g. only small dogs accepted)*
- ○ Number restrictions *(max. 1 or 2 dogs)*
- ☑ Dog sanitary facilities *(e.g. waste bins, bags)*
- ☑ Dog showers
- ☑ On-site dog walking area
- ○ Kennels
- ☑ Vet nearby *(able to help with UK Pet Passports)*

Camping Sobec

Sobceva cesta 25, SLO-4248 Lesce
t: 045 353 700 e: sobec@siol.net
alanrogers.com/SV4210 www.sobec.si

Accommodation: ☑ Pitch ☑ Mobile home/chalet ○ Hotel/B&B ○ Apartment

Sobec is situated in a valley between the Julian Alps and the Karavanke Mountains, in a pine grove between the Sava Dolinka river and a small lake. It is only 3 km. from Bled and 20 km. from the Karavanke Tunnel. There are 500 unmarked pitches on level, grassy fields off tarmac access roads (450 for touring units), all with 16A electricity. Shade is provided by mature pine trees and younger trees separate some pitches. Camping Sobec is surrounded by water – the Sava river borders it on three sides and on the fourth is a small, artificial lake with grassy fields for sunbathing. Some pitches have views over the lake, which has an enclosed area providing safe swimming for children. This site is a good base for an active holiday, since both the Sava Dolinka and the Sava Bohinjka rivers are suitable for canoeing, kayaking, rafting and fishing, whilst the nearby mountains offer challenges for mountain climbing, paragliding and canyoning.

Facilities: Three traditional style toilet blocks (all now refurbished) with mainly British style toilets, washbasins in cabins and controllable hot showers. Child size toilets and basins. Well equipped baby room. Facilities for disabled visitors. Laundry facilities. Motorcaravan service point. Supermarket, bar/restaurant with stage for live performances. Playgrounds. Rafting, canyoning and kayaking organised. Miniclub. Tours to Bled and the Triglav National Park organised. WiFi throughout (free). Off site: Golf and riding 2 km.

Open: 14 April - 30 September.

Directions: Site is off the main road from Lesce to Bled and is well signed just outside Lesce.
GPS: 46.35607, 14.14992

Charges guide

Per unit incl. 2 persons and electricity	€ 24,70 - € 30,10
extra person	€ 10,60 - € 13,30
child (7-14 yrs)	€ 7,90 - € 9,90
dog	€ 3,50

You might like to know

The village of Lesce, 2 km. away, is accessible by road or you take the shorter path through the forest.

- ☑ Dogs welcome *(subject to conditions)*
- ☑ Dogs welcome all season
- ○ Dogs welcome part season
- ○ Breed restrictions *(e.g. only small dogs accepted)*
- ☑ Number restrictions *(max. 1 or 2 dogs)*
- ○ Dog sanitary facilities *(e.g. waste bins, bags)*
- ○ Dog showers
- ○ On-site dog walking area
- ○ Kennels
- ○ Vet nearby *(able to help with UK Pet Passports)*

Facilities: Two toilet blocks (one new) have modern fittings with toilets, open plan washbasins and controllable hot showers. Motorcaravan service point. Bar/restaurant with open-air terrace (evenings only) and open-air kitchen. Sauna. Playing field. Play area. Fishing. Mountain bike hire. Russian bowling. Excursions (52). Live music and gatherings around the camp fire. Indian village. Hostel. Skiing in winter. Kayaking. Mobile homes to rent. Climbing wall. Rafting. Off site: Fishing 2 km. Recica and other villages with much culture and folklore are close. Indian sauna at Coze.

Open: All year.

Directions: From Ljubljana/Celje autobahn A1. Exit at Sentupert and turn north towards Mozirje (14 km). At roundabout just before Mozirje, hard left staying on the 225 for 6 km. to Nizka then just after the circular automatic petrol station, left where site is signed.

GPS: 46.31168, 14.90913

Charges guide

Per unit incl. 2 persons
and electricity € 17,80 - € 23,00

extra person € 7,50 - € 10,00

child (5-15 yrs) € 3,50 - € 6,00

dog € 2,50 - € 3,00

Slovenia – Recica ob Savinji

Camping Menina

Varpolje 105, SLO-3332 Recica ob Savinji
t: 035 835 027   e: info@campingmenina.com
alanrogers.com/SV4405   www.campingmenina.com

Accommodation: ☑ Pitch   ☑ Mobile home/chalet   ○ Hotel/B&B   ○ Apartment

Camping Menina is in the heart of the 35 km. long Upper Savinja Valley, surrounded by 2,500 m. high mountains and unspoilt nature. It is being improved every year by the young, enthusiastic owner, Jurij Kolenc and has 200 pitches, all for touring units, on grassy fields under mature trees and with access from gravel roads. All have 6-10A electricity. The Savinja river runs along one side of the site, but if its water is too cold for swimming, the site also has a lake which can be used for swimming. This site is a perfect base for walking or mountain biking in the mountains. A wealth of maps and routes are available from reception. Rafting, canyoning and kayaking, and visits to a fitness studio, sauna and massage salon are organised. The site is now open all year to offer skiing holidays.

You might like to know

This is great walking country. For more experienced hikers, there are a number of peaks over 2,000 m. surrounding the Logar Valley.

- ☑ Dogs welcome *(subject to conditions)*
- ☑ Dogs welcome all season
- ○ Dogs welcome part season
- ○ Breed restrictions *(e.g. only small dogs accepted)*
- ☑ Number restrictions *(max. 1 or 2 dogs)*
- ○ Dog sanitary facilities *(e.g. waste bins, bags)*
- ○ Dog showers
- ○ On-site dog walking area
- ○ Kennels
- ○ Vet nearby *(able to help with UK Pet Passports)*

Facilities: Two modern toilet blocks with British style toilets, washbasins in cabins, large and controllable hot showers. Child sized washbasins. Facilities for disabled visitors. Laundry facilities. Motorcaravan service point. Supermarket. Kiosks for fruit, newspapers, souvenirs and tobacco. Attractive restaurant with buffet. Bar with terrace. Large indoor and outdoor swimming complexes. Rowing boats. Jogging track. Fishing. Golf. Bicycle hire. Sauna. Solarium. Riding. Organised activities. Video games. WiFi throughout (free). Off site: Golf 7 km.

Open: All year.

Directions: Site is signed from the Ljubljana-Zagreb motorway (E70) 6 km. west of the Slovenia/Croatia border, close to Brezice.

GPS: 45.89137, 15.62598

Charges guide

Per unit incl. 2 persons and electricity	€ 40,30 - € 49,50
extra person	€ 17,90 - € 22,50
child (4-11 yrs)	€ 8,95 - € 11,25
dog	€ 4,00

Slovenia – Catez ob Savi

Camping Terme Catez

Topliska cesta 35, SLO-8251 Catez ob Savi
t: 074 936 700   e: info@terme-catez.si
alanrogers.com/SV4415   www.terme-catez.si

Accommodation: ☑ Pitch   ☑ Mobile home/chalet   ○ Hotel/B&B   ○ Apartment

Terme Catez is part of the modern Catez thermal spa, which includes very large and attractive indoor (31ºC) and outdoor swimming complexes, both with large slides and waves. The campsite has 450 pitches, with 190 places for tourers, arranged on one large, open field, with some young trees – a real sun trap – and provides level, grass pitches which are numbered by markings on the tarmac access roads. All have 10A electricity connections. Although the site is ideally placed for an overnight stop when travelling on the E70, it is well worthwhile planning to spend some time here to take advantage of the excellent facilities that are included in the overnight camping charges. The site is in the centre of a large complex which caters for most needs with its pools, large shopping centre, gym and the numerous events that are organised, such as the Magic School and Junior Olympic Games for children.

You might like to know

A wide range of leisure facilities is on offer here, including several swimming pools.

- ☑ Dogs welcome *(subject to conditions)*
- ☑ Dogs welcome all season
- ○ Dogs welcome part season
- ○ Breed restrictions *(e.g. only small dogs accepted)*
- ☑ Number restrictions *(max. 1 or 2 dogs)*
- ○ Dog sanitary facilities *(e.g. waste bins, bags)*
- ○ Dog showers
- ○ On-site dog walking area
- ○ Kennels
- ○ Vet nearby *(able to help with UK Pet Passports)*

Facilities:
Seven separate toilet blocks are practical, heated and fully equipped. They include free hot water for baths and showers. Twenty private toilet units are for rent. Laundry facilities. Motorcaravan services. Gas supplies. Excellent shop (1/4-15/10). Site-owned restaurant adjacent (1/3-30/10). Snack bar with takeaway (1/7-20/8). TV room. Playground and paddling pool. Minigolf. Bicycle hire. Sailing school. Lake swimming. Boat hire (slipway for campers' own). Fishing. Daily activity and entertainment programme in high season. Excursions. Max. 1 dog. WiFi (charged). Off site: Golf (18 holes) 500 m. (handicap card). Riding 3 km. Good area for cycling and walking. Free return bus and boat service to Interlaken's stations and heated indoor and outdoor swimming pools (free entry).

Open: All year.

Directions: Site is 3 km. west of Interlaken along the road running north of the Thuner See towards Thun. Follow signs for 'Camp 1'. From A8 (bypassing Interlaken) take exit 24 marked 'Gunten, Beatenberg', which is a spur road bringing you out close to site.
GPS: 46.68129, 7.81524

Charges guide

Per unit incl. 2 persons and electricity	CHF 37,00 - 63,50
extra person	CHF 10,50
child (6-15 yrs)	CHF 5,00
dog	CHF 4,00

Various discounts for longer stays.

Camping Manor Farm 1

Seestrassee 201, Unterseen, CH-3800 Interlaken-Thunersee (Bern)
t: 033 822 2264   e: info@manorfarm.ch
alanrogers.com/CH9420   www.manorfarm.ch

Accommodation: ☑ Pitch   ☑ Mobile home/chalet   ○ Hotel/B&B   ☑ Apartment

Manor Farm has been popular with British visitors for many years, as this is one of the traditional touring areas of Switzerland. The flat terrain is divided into 500 individual, numbered pitches, which vary considerably, both in size (60-100 sq.m) and price. There is shade in some places. There are 144 pitches with electricity (4/13A), water and drainage, and 55 also have cable TV connections. Reservations can be made, although you should find space, except perhaps in late July/early August when the best places may be taken. Around 40 per cent of the pitches are taken by permanent or letting units and four tour operators. The site lies outside the town on the northern side of the Thuner See, with most of the site between the road and lake but with one part on the far side of the road. Interlaken is very much a tourist town, but the area is rich in scenery with innumerable mountain excursions and walks available. The lakes and Jungfrau railway are near at hand. Manor Farm is a large campsite, efficiently run with a minimum of formality and would suit those looking for an active family holiday.

You might like to know
Manor Farm is one of Switzerland's best known sites. This south-facing campsite is surrounded by dramatic mountains with views towards the Bernese Oberland.

- ☑ Dogs welcome *(subject to conditions)*
- ☑ Dogs welcome all season
- ○ Dogs welcome part season
- ○ Breed restrictions *(e.g. only small dogs accepted)*
- ☑ Number restrictions *(max. 1 or 2 dogs)*
- ○ Dog sanitary facilities *(e.g. waste bins, bags)*
- ○ Dog showers
- ○ On-site dog walking area
- ○ Kennels
- ○ Vet nearby *(able to help with UK Pet Passports)*

Facilities:
Two good sanitary blocks are both heated with free hot showers, good facilities for disabled campers and a baby room. Laundry. Campers' kitchen with microwave, cooker, fridge and utensils. Motorcaravan service point. Well stocked shop. TV and games room. Play area. Small swimming pool and hot tub (all season). Wooden igloos and bungalows for rent. Free WiFi. Free bus in the Interlaken area – bus stop is five minutes walk from site. Off site: Cycle trails and waymarked footpaths. Riding and bicycle hire 500 m. Golf 1 km. Fishing 1 km. Boat launching 1.5 km. Interlaken and leisure centre 2 km.

Open: 18 April - 20 October.

Directions: Site is on north side of Lake Thun. From road 8 (Thun-Interlaken) on south side of lake take exit 24 Interlaken West. Follow towards lake at roundabout then follow signs for campings. Lazy Rancho is Camp 4. The last 500 m. is a little narrow but no problem.

GPS: 46.68605, 7.830633

Charges guide

Per unit incl. 2 persons
and electricity CHF 30,50 - 54,50

extra person CHF 6,00 - 8,00

child (6-15 yrs) CHF 3,50 - 4,80

dog no charge - CHF 3,00

Payment also accepted in euros.

Camping Lazy Rancho 4

Lehnweg 6, CH-3800 Unterseen-Interlaken (Bern)
t: 033 822 8716 e: info@lazyrancho.ch
alanrogers.com/CH9430 www.lazyrancho.ch

Accommodation: ◉ Pitch ◉ Mobile home/chalet ○ Hotel/B&B ○ Apartment

This super site is in a quiet location with fantastic views of the dramatic mountains of Eiger, Monch and Jungfrau. Neat, orderly and well maintained, the site is situated in a wide valley just 1 km. from Lake Thun and 1.5 km. from Interlaken. The English speaking owners lovingly care for the site and will endeavour to make you feel very welcome. Connected by gravel roads, the 155 pitches, of which 90 are for touring units, are on well tended level grass (some with hardstanding, all with 10A electricity). There are 28 pitches also with water and waste water drainage. This is a quiet, friendly site, popular with British visitors. The owners offer advice on day trips out, and how to get the best bargains on the railway.

You might like to know
One of the best ways to discover the spectacular sights of the Jungfrau region is on the Jungfrau mountain railway.

- ◉ Dogs welcome *(subject to conditions)*
- ◉ Dogs welcome all season
- ○ Dogs welcome part season
- ○ Breed restrictions *(e.g. only small dogs accepted)*
- ◉ Number restrictions *(max. 1 or 2 dogs)*
- ○ Dog sanitary facilities *(e.g. waste bins, bags)*
- ○ Dog showers
- ○ On-site dog walking area
- ○ Kennels
- ○ Vet nearby *(able to help with UK Pet Passports)*

Camping Aaregg

Seestrasse 28a, CH-3855 Brienz am See (Bern)
t: 033 951 1843   e: mail@aaregg.ch
alanrogers.com/CH9510   www.aaregg.ch

Accommodation: ⦿ Pitch   ⦿ Mobile home/chalet   ○ Hotel/B&B   ○ Apartment

Brienz, in the Bernese Oberland, is a delightful little town on the lake of the same name and the centre of the Swiss wood carving industry. Camping Aaregg is an excellent site situated on the southern shores of the lake with splendid views across the water to the mountains. There are 65 static caravans occupying their own area and 180 touring pitches, all with electricity (10/16A). Of these, 16 are larger with hardstandings, water and drainage and many of these have good lake views. Pitches fronting the lake have a surcharge. The trees and flowers make an attractive and peaceful environment. An excellent base from which to explore the many attractions of this scenic region, and a useful night stop when passing from Interlaken to Luzern. Nearby at Ballenberg is the fascinating Freilichtmuseum, a very large open-air park of old Swiss houses which have been brought from all over Switzerland and re-erected in groups. Traditional Swiss crafts are demonstrated in some of these.

You might like to know

This is a friendly family campsite on the banks of the beautiful Brienzersee, with some great spots for dog walking.

⦿ Dogs welcome *(subject to conditions)*

⦿ Dogs welcome all season

○ Dogs welcome part season

○ Breed restrictions *(e.g. only small dogs accepted)*

⦿ Number restrictions *(max. 1 or 2 dogs)*

⦿ Dog sanitary facilities *(e.g. waste bins, bags)*

○ Dog showers

○ On-site dog walking area

○ Kennels

○ Vet nearby *(able to help with UK Pet Passports)*

Facilities: New, very attractive sanitary facilities built and maintained to first class standards. Showers with washbasins. Washbasins (open style and in cubicles). Children's section. Family shower rooms. Baby changing room. Facilities for disabled visitors. Laundry facilities. Motorcaravan services. Pleasant restaurant with terrace and takeaway in season. Play area. Fishing. Bicycle hire. Boat launching. Lake swimming in clear water (unsupervised). English is spoken. Off site: Frequent train services to Interlaken and Lucerne as well as boat cruises from Brienz to Interlaken and back. Motorboat hire is possible, and water skiing on the lake.

Open: 1 April - 31 October.

Directions: Site is on road B6/B11 on the east of Brienz. Entrance is just opposite the Esso filling station, well signed. From the Interlaken-Luzern motorway, take Brienz exit and turn towards Brienz, site then on the left.

GPS: 46.7483, 8.04871

Charges guide

Per unit incl. 2 persons and electricity	CHF 39,20 - 56,00
extra person	CHF 7,70 - 11,00
child (6-16 yrs)	CHF 4,90 - 7,00
dog	CHF 4,00

Low season less 10%.

Camping Eienwäldli

Wasserfallstrasse 108, CH-6390 Engelberg (Unterwalden)
t: 041 637 1949   e: info@eienwaeldli.ch
alanrogers.com/CH9570   www.eienwaeldli.ch

Accommodation: ☑ Pitch   ☑ Mobile home/chalet   ☑ Hotel/B&B   ○ Apartment

Facilities: The main toilet block, heated in cool weather, is situated at the rear of the hotel and has free hot water in washbasins (in cabins) and (charged) showers. A new modern toilet block has been added near the top end of the site. Washing machines and dryers. Shop. Café/bar. Small lounge. Indoor pool complex. Ski facilities including a drying room. Large play area with a rafting pool fed by fresh water from the mountain stream. Torches useful. TV. WiFi. Golf. Off site: Golf driving range and 18-hole course nearby. Fishing and bicycle hire 1 km. Riding 2 km.

Open: All year.

Directions: From N2 Gotthard motorway, leave at exit 33 Stans-Sud and follow signs to Engelberg. Turn right at T-junction on edge of town and follow signs to 'Wasserfall' and site.
GPS: 46.80940, 8.42367

Charges guide

Per person CHF 6,90 - 11,00	
child (6-15 yrs) CHF 4,25 - 5,50	
pitch incl. electricity (plus meter) CHF 10,00 - 17,00	
dog CHF 2,00	

Credit cards accepted (surcharge).

This super site has facilities which must make it one of the best in Switzerland. It is situated in a beautiful location, 3,500 feet above sea level, surrounded by mountains on the edge of the delightful village of Engelberg. Half of the site is taken up by static caravans which are grouped together at one side. The camping area is in two parts – nearest the entrance there are 57 hardstandings for caravans and motorcaravans, all with electricity (metered), and beyond this is a flat meadow for about 70 tents. Reception can be found in the very modern foyer of the Eienwäldli Hotel which also houses the indoor pool, health complex, shop and café/bar. The indoor pool has been most imaginatively rebuilt as a Felsenbad spa bath with adventure pool, steam and relaxing grottoes, Kneipp's cure, children's pool with water slides, solarium, Finnish sauna and eucalyptus steam bath (charged for). Being about 35 km. from Luzern by road and with a rail link, it makes a quiet, peaceful base from which to explore the Vierwaldstattersee region, walk in the mountains or just enjoy the scenery.

You might like to know

A maximum of one dog per pitch is allowed at this site.

- ☑ Dogs welcome *(subject to conditions)*
- ☑ Dogs welcome all season
- ○ Dogs welcome part season
- ○ Breed restrictions *(e.g. only small dogs accepted)*
- ☑ Number restrictions *(max. 1 or 2 dogs)*
- ○ Dog sanitary facilities *(e.g. waste bins, bags)*
- ○ Dog showers
- ○ On-site dog walking area
- ○ Kennels
- ○ Vet nearby *(able to help with UK Pet Passports)*

Facilities: Good sanitary facilities are in a small building near reception and a larger unit halfway up the site. Curtained, hot showers with curtained communal changing. Cooking facilities. Bar and meals (1/6-31/8). Shop. Recreation room with TV and games. Small play area and small pool (cleaned once a week). No charcoal barbecues. No English is spoken. Off site: Hourly bus service to Györ. Shop for essentials 150 m. Good value restaurant 400 m. away in the village. Riding 3 km. Fishing 4 km.

Open: 1 May - 31 August.

Directions: From no. 82 Györ-Veszprém road turn to Pannonhalma at Ecs. Site is well signed – the final approach road is fairly steep.

GPS: 47.54915, 17.7578

Charges guide

Per unit incl. 2 persons and electricity	HUF 4900
extra person	HUF 1000
child (2-14 yrs)	HUF 500
dog	HUF 450

No credit cards.

Panoráma Camping

Fenyvesalja 4/A, H-9090 Pannonhalma (Györ-Moson-Sopron County)
t: 96 471 240 e: info@borbirodalum.hu
alanrogers.com/HU5130

Accommodation: ◉ Pitch ○ Mobile home/chalet ◉ Hotel/B&B ○ Apartment

In 1982 this became the first private enterprise campsite in Hungary. It offers a very pleasant outlook and peaceful stay at the start or end of your visit to this country, situated just 20 km. southeast of Györ, on a hillside with views across the valley to the Sokoro hills. The 70 numbered and hedged touring pitches (50 with 16A electricity, long leads necessary) are on terraces, generally fairly level but reached by fairly steep concrete access roads, with many trees and plants around. Some small hardstandings are provided. There are benches provided and a small, grass terrace below reception from where you can purchase beer, local wine and soft drinks, etc. Occasional big stews are cooked in high season and the wine cellar in the village is recommended. On the edge of the village, it is just below the 1,000-year-old Benedictine monastery, which has guided tours and a library of some 300,000 books. The site has its own stairway up to the monastery. At exactly ten o'clock, the last post can be heard and this means the site is officially closed for the night.

You might like to know

This site is attractively located beneath the arboretum surrounding the Benedictine Abbey, with fine views of the building.

- ◉ Dogs welcome *(subject to conditions)*
- ◉ Dogs welcome all season
- ○ Dogs welcome part season
- ◉ Breed restrictions *(e.g. only small dogs accepted)*
- ◉ Number restrictions *(max. 1 or 2 dogs)*
- ○ Dog sanitary facilities *(e.g. waste bins, bags)*
- ○ Dog showers
- ○ On-site dog walking area
- ○ Kennels
- ○ Vet nearby *(able to help with UK Pet Passports)*

Balatontourist Camping Napfény

Halász ut. 5, H-8253 Révfülöp (Veszprem County)
t: 87 563 031   e: napfeny@balatontourist.hu
alanrogers.com/HU5370   www.balatontourist.hu

Accommodation: ☑ Pitch   ☑ Mobile home/chalet   ○ Hotel/B&B   ○ Apartment

Facilities: The three excellent sanitary blocks have toilets, washbasins (open style and in cabins) with hot and cold water, spacious showers (both preset and controllable), child size toilets and basins, and two bathrooms (hourly charge). Heated baby room. Facilities for disabled campers. Launderette. Dog shower. Motorcaravan services. Supermarket, souvenir shop and several bars (all 1/6-31/8). Restaurants. Children's pool. Sports field. Minigolf. Fishing. Bicycle hire. Canoe, rowing boat and pedalo hire. Extensive entertainment programme for all ages. WiFi throughout (charged). Off site: Tennis 300 m. Riding 3 km. Golf 20 km.

Open: 27 April - 30 September.

Directions: Follow road 71 from Veszprém southeast to Keszthely. Site is in Révfülöp.

GPS: 46.829469, 17.640164

Charges guide

Per unit incl. 2 persons and electricity	HUF 3600 - 7150
extra person	HUF 850 - 1200
child (2-14 yrs)	HUF 550 - 950
dog	HUF 550 - 950

Camping Napfény, an exceptionally good site, is designed for families with children of all ages looking for an active holiday, and has a 200 m. frontage on Lake Balaton. The site's 370 pitches vary in size (60-110 sq.m) and almost all have shade – very welcome during the hot Hungarian summers – and 6-10A electricity. As with most of the sites on Lake Balaton, a train line runs just outside the site boundary. There are steps to get into the lake and canoes, boats and pedaloes for hire. An extensive entertainment programme is designed for all ages and there are several bars and restaurants of various styles. There are souvenir shops and a supermarket. In fact, you need not leave the site at all during your holiday, although there are several excursions on offer, including to Budapest or to one of the many Hungarian spas, a trip over Lake Balaton or a traditional wine tour.

You might like to know

Lake Balaton provides some great opportunities for you and your dog to enjoy a walk.

- ☑ Dogs welcome *(subject to conditions)*
- ☑ Dogs welcome all season
- ○ Dogs welcome part season
- ☑ Breed restrictions *(e.g. only small dogs accepted)*
- ☑ Number restrictions *(max. 1 or 2 dogs)*
- ☑ Dog sanitary facilities *(e.g. waste bins, bags)*
- ☑ Dog showers
- ○ On-site dog walking area
- ○ Kennels
- ○ Vet nearby *(able to help with UK Pet Passports)*

Facilities:
A good sanitary block provides some washbasins in cabins and 20 private bathrooms for rent. Separate baby and toddler unit. Facilities for disabled visitors. Laundry facilities. Drying rooms. Motorcaravan service point. Dog washing area. Shop. Bar. Restaurant. Indoor pool with sauna, whirlpool and fitness centre with solarium and massage room. Outdoor pool and children's pool with slide. Internet access. Bicycle loan and motor scooters for hire. Play area. Organised activities in season. Off site: Hotel, souvenir shop and cable car station 100 m. Sports in Ehrwald 5 km.

Open: 1 January - Easter, 28 May - 31 October, mid - end December.

Directions: Carefully follow signs in Ehrwald to Tiroler Zugspitzbahn and then signs to site.

GPS: 47.42521, 10.93809

Charges guide

Per person € 8,00 - € 18,00	
child (4-15 yrs) € 5,00 - € 12,00	
pitch € 9,00 - € 14,00	
electricity per kWh € 0,80	
dog € 4,00	

Special seasonal weekly offers.

Ferienanlage Tiroler Zugspitze

Obermoos 1, A-6632 Ehrwald (Tirol)
t: 056 732 309 e: welcome@zugspitze-resort.at
alanrogers.com/AU0040 www.zugspitze-resort.at

Accommodation: ☑ Pitch ○ Mobile home/chalet ☑ Hotel/B&B ☑ Apartment

Although Ehrwald is in Austria, it is from the entrance of Tiroler Zugspitze that a cable car runs to the summit of Germany's highest mountain. Standing at 1,200 feet above sea level at the foot of the mountain, the 200 pitches (120 for touring), mainly of stones over grass, are on flat terraces with fine panoramic views in parts. All have 16A electricity connections. The modern reception building at the entrance also houses a fine restaurant with a terrace which is open to those using the cable car, as well as those staying on the site. There are some 30 pitches outside the barrier for late arrivals and overnighters. A further large modern building, heated in cool weather, has indoor and outdoor pools, sauna, mini-gym and wellness centre. This excellent mountain site, with its superb facilities, provides a good base from which to explore this interesting part of Austria and Bavaria by car or on foot. A trip up to the Zugspitze offers beautiful views and opportunities for mountain walking.

You might like to know

There are forest walks and mountain hikes in the immediate area, so plenty of opportunities for exercising your dog.

- ☑ Dogs welcome *(subject to conditions)*
- ☑ Dogs welcome all season
- ○ Dogs welcome part season
- ○ Breed restrictions *(e.g. only small dogs accepted)*
- ☑ Number restrictions *(max. 1 or 2 dogs)*
- ○ Dog sanitary facilities *(e.g. waste bins, bags)*
- ☑ Dog showers
- ○ On-site dog walking area
- ○ Kennels
- ○ Vet nearby *(able to help with UK Pet Passports)*

Ferienparadies Natterer See

Natterer See 1, A-6161 Natters (Tirol)
t: 051 254 6732   e: info@natterersee.com
alanrogers.com/AU0060   www.natterersee.com

Accommodation: ◉ Pitch   ○ Mobile home/chalet   ○ Hotel/B&B   ◉ Apartment

Facilities: The large sanitary block has underfloor heating, some private cabins, plus excellent facilities for babies, children and disabled visitors. Laundry facilities. Motorcaravan services. Fridge box hire. Bar. Restaurant and takeaway with at least one open all year. Pizzeria. Good shop. Playgrounds. Children's activity programme. Child minding (day nursery) in high season. Sports field. Archery. Youth room with games, pool and billiards. TV room with Sky. Open-air cinema. Mountain bike hire. Aquapark (1/5-30/9). Surf bikes and pedaloes. Canoes and mini sailboats for rent. Fishing. Extensive daily entertainment programme (mid May-mid Oct). Dogs are not accepted in high season (July/Aug). WiFi (charged). Off site: Tennis and minigolf nearby. Riding 6 km. Golf 12 km.

Open: All year.

Directions: From Inntal autobahn (A12) take Brenner autobahn (A13) as far as Innsbruck-sud/Natters exit (no. 3). Turn left by Shell petrol station onto B182 to Natters. At roundabout take first exit and immediately right again and follow signs to site 4 km. Do not use sat nav for final approach to site, follow camping signs.

GPS: 47.23755, 11.34201

Charges guide

Per unit incl. 2 persons and electricity	€ 24,45 - € 33,25
extra person	€ 6,10 - € 9,00
child (under 13 yrs)	€ 4,80 - € 6,50
dog (excl. July/Aug)	€ 4,50 - € 5,00

Special weekly, winter, summer or Christmas packages.

In a quiet location arranged around two lakes and set amidst beautiful alpine scenery, this site founded in 1930 is renowned as one of Austria's top sites. Over the last few years many improvements have been carried out and pride of place goes to the innovative, award-winning, multifunctional building at the entrance to the site. This contains all of the sanitary facilities expected of a top site, including a special section for children, private bathrooms to rent and also a dog bath. The reception, shop, café/bar/bistro and cinema are on the ground floor, and on the upper floor is a panoramic lounge. Almost all of the 235 pitches are for tourers. They are terraced, set on gravel/grass, all have electricity and most offer a splendid view of the mountains. The site's lakeside restaurant with bar and large terrace has a good menu and is the ideal place to spend the evening. With a bus every hour and the city centre only 19 minutes away this is also a good site from which to visit Innsbruck. The Innsbruck Card is available at reception and allows free bus transport in the city, including a sightseeing tour, free entry to museums and one cable car trip.

You might like to know

Woodland, mountain and alpine pastures are all in the immediate area and are suitable for dog walking. Dogs are allowed in caravan accommodation all year round.

- ◉ Dogs welcome *(subject to conditions)*
- ○ Dogs welcome all season
- ◉ Dogs welcome part season
- ○ Breed restrictions *(e.g. only small dogs accepted)*
- ◉ Number restrictions *(max. 1 or 2 dogs)*
- ○ Dog sanitary facilities *(e.g. waste bins, bags)*
- ◉ Dog showers
- ○ On-site dog walking area
- ○ Kennels
- ○ Vet nearby *(able to help with UK Pet Passports)*

Facilities:
Five well kept, heated sanitary blocks of excellent quality and size, each with a few washbasins in cabins for each sex, baby rooms and nine units for disabled visitors. Four additional units provide 40 private bathrooms for luxury pitches and several family bathrooms for rent. Laundry and drying rooms. Ski room. Motorcaravan services. Supermarket. Restaurant. General room. TV. Indoor pool, sauna and sun beds. Wellness centre. Outdoor pool. Playground. Multisport court. Tennis. Riding. Skateboard and rollerblade facilities. Trampolines. Bicycle hire. WiFi (charged). ATM. Western village. Entertainment in high season includes line dancing, Western shows and archery. Ski slope and lift. Off site: Walking and cycling in the Zillertall valley. Cross-country skiing (winter). Active club in front of site free to campers. Golf 7 km. Fishing 10 km.

Open: All year excl. 3 November - 8 December.

Directions: From A12 Inntal motorway, take Zillertal exit 39, 32 km. northeast of Innsbruck. Follow road no. 169 to village of Aschau from which site is well signed.
GPS: 47.263333, 11.899333

Charges guide
Per unit incl. 2 persons,
electricity on meter € 20,40 - € 35,70

incl. private sanitary cabin	€ 28,80 - € 50,60
extra person	€ 6,50 - € 11,90
child (2-12 yrs)	€ 5,00 - € 8,10
dog	€ 5,00

Winter prices are higher.

Erlebnis-Comfort-Camping Aufenfeld

Aufenfeldweg 10, A-6274 Aschau im Zillertal (Tirol)
t: 052 822 9160 e: info@camping-zillertal.at
alanrogers.com/AU0120 www.camping-zillertal.at

Accommodation: ◉ Pitch ◉ Mobile home/chalet ○ Hotel/B&B ◉ Apartment

This outstanding site is situated in a wide mountain valley with fine views and first class facilities. The main area of the site itself is flat with pitches up to 100 sq.m. on grass and gravel, between hard access roads, with further pitches on terraces at the rear. There are 350 pitches (240 for touring units with 6A electricity) including 40 with private bathrooms. The site can become full mid July until mid August and at Christmas. A splendid indoor swimming pool has been added and there is a heated outdoor pool, paddling pool, and tennis courts for summer use, as well as a play and activity centre. A ski lift and gentle slope are on site in winter, with horse riding on site in summer. A comprehensive wellness centre provides super fitness, massage and spa facilities with an imaginative Western theme. A lake and leisure area has been created alongside the site, together with a Western village for children. There are around 60 privately owned or rental units and 50 seasonal units on site. Note: pylons and power lines cross the site over some pitches. A member of Leading Campings group.

You might like to know

There are over 1,000 km, of walking trails in the Zillertal – heaven on earth for ambitious walkers and their dogs!

- ◉ Dogs welcome *(subject to conditions)*
- ◉ Dogs welcome all season
- ○ Dogs welcome part season
- ◉ Breed restrictions *(e.g. only small dogs accepted)*
- ◉ Number restrictions *(max. 1 or 2 dogs)*
- ◉ Dog sanitary facilities *(e.g. waste bins, bags)*
- ○ Dog showers
- ◉ On-site dog walking area
- ○ Kennels
- ◉ Vet nearby *(able to help with UK Pet Passports)*

Aktiv-Camping Prutz Tirol

Pontlatzstrasse 22, A-6522 Prutz (Tirol)
t: 054 722 648   e: info@aktiv-camping.at
alanrogers.com/AU0155   www.aktiv-camping.at

Accommodation: ☑ Pitch   ○ Mobile home/chalet   ○ Hotel/B&B   ○ Apartment

Aktiv-Camping is a long site which lies beside, but is fenced off from, the River Inn. The 115 touring pitches, mainly gravelled for motorcaravans, are on level ground and average 80 sq.m. They all have 6A electrical connections, adequate water points, and in the larger area fit together somewhat informally. As a result, the site can sometimes have the appearance of being quite crowded. This is an attractive area with many activities in both summer and winter for all age groups. You may well consider using this site not just as an overnight stop, but also for a longer stay. From Roman times onwards, when the Via Augusta passed through, this border region's strategic importance has left behind many fortifications that today feature among its many tourist attractions. Others include rambling, cycling and mountain biking, swimming in lakes and pools as well as interesting, educational and adventurous activities for children. The Tiroler Summer card, available without charge at reception, has free offers and discounts for many attractions; in addition the booklet Wonderful Holiday Bliss, free at reception, contains a wealth of useful tourist information.

Facilities: The sanitary facilities are of a very high standard, with private cabins and good facilities for disabled visitors. Baby room. Washing machine. Dog shower. Small shop (all year). Bar, restaurant and takeaway (15/5-30/9; Christmas to Easter). Play room. Ski room. Play area. Children's entertainment. Guided walks. Free shuttle bus to ski slopes. Bicycle hire. Slipway for canoes/kayaks. WiFi over site. Off site: Riding 1 km. Indoor pool at Feichten, Pilgrim's Church at Kaltenbrunn. Kaunertaler Glacier.

Open: All year.

Directions: From E60/A12 exit at Landeck and follow the B315 (direction Reschenpass) turn south onto the B180 signed Bregenz, Arlberg, Innsbruck and Fern Pass for 11 km. to Prutz. Site is signed to the right from the B180 over the bridge.
GPS: 47.08033, 10.659698

Charges guide

Per unit incl. 2 persons
and electricity € 17,00 - € 27,00

extra person	€ 4,20 - € 7,50
child (5-17 yrs)	€ 3,80 - € 6,20
dog	€ 2,00 - € 3,00

You might like to know

This site is open all year round, so good for a winter holiday too.

- ☑ **Dogs welcome** (subject to conditions)
- ☑ **Dogs welcome all season**
- ○ **Dogs welcome part season**
- ○ **Breed restrictions** (e.g. only small dogs accepted)
- ☑ **Number restrictions** (max. 1 or 2 dogs)
- ○ **Dog sanitary facilities** (e.g. waste bins, bags)
- ☑ **Dog showers**
- ○ **On-site dog walking area**
- ○ **Kennels**
- ○ **Vet nearby** (able to help with UK Pet Passports)

Facilities: Three modern sanitary blocks (the newest in a class of its own) have excellent facilities, including private cabins, underfloor heating and music. Washing machines and dryers. Facilities for disabled visitors. Family bathrooms for hire (some with bathtubs). Motorcaravan services. Well stocked shop. Bar, restaurant and takeaway. Small, heated outdoor pool and children's pool (1/5-15/10). Fitness centre. Two playgrounds, indoor play room and children's cinema. Tennis. Bicycle hire. Watersports and lake swimming. Children's farm and pony rides. New crazy golf course. WiFi over site (charged). Off site: ATM 500 m. Fishing 100 m. Riding 1.5 km. Golf 3 km. Boat launching and sailing 3.5 km. Hiking and skiing nearby. Dry toboggan run at Kaprun 4 km.

Open: All year.

Directions: Site is southwest of Bruck. From road B311, Bruck bypass, take southern exit (Grossglockner) and site is signed from the junction of B311 and B107 roads (small signs). Note: 3.4 m. height restriction if you go through village.
GPS: 47.2838, 12.81694

Charges guide

Per unit incl. 2 persons and electricity (plus meter)	€ 23,80 - € 33,90
extra person	€ 5,60 - € 9,00
child (2-10 yrs)	€ 4,40 - € 6,60
dog	€ 3,40 - € 4,60

Special offers for longer stays in low season.

Austria – Bruck

Sportcamp Woferlgut

Kroessenbach 40, A-5671 Bruck (Salzburg)
t: 065 457 3030 e: info@sportcamp.at
alanrogers.com/AU0180 www.sportcamp.at

Accommodation: ☑ Pitch ☑ Mobile home/chalet ☑ Hotel/B&B ☑ Apartment

The village of Bruck lies at the northern end of the Grossglocknerstrasse spectacular mountain road in the Hohe Tauern National Park, very near the Zeller See. Sportcamp Woferlgut, a family run site, is one of the very best in Austria. Surrounded by mountains, the site is quite flat with pleasant views. The 520 level, grass pitches (300 for touring units) are marked out by shrubs and each has 16A electricity (Europlug), water, drainage, cable TV socket and gas point. A high grass bank separates the site from the road. The site's own lake, used for swimming, is surrounded by a landscaped sunbathing area. A free activity and entertainment programme is provided all year round, but especially during the summer. This includes live music evenings, a club for children, weekly barbecues and guided cycle and mountain tours. The fitness centre has a fully equipped gym, whilst another building contains a sauna and cold dip, Turkish bath, solarium (all free), massage (charged), and a bar. In winter, a cross-country skiing trail and toboggan run lead from the site and a free bus service is provided to nearby skiing facilities. A member of Leading Campings group.

You might like to know

The site is surrounded by alpine pastures and wooded areas that are ideal for dog walking. The national park is nearby and is excellent for hiking.

- ☑ Dogs welcome *(subject to conditions)*
- ☑ Dogs welcome all season
- ○ Dogs welcome part season
- ○ Breed restrictions *(e.g. only small dogs accepted)*
- ☑ Number restrictions *(max. 1 or 2 dogs)*
- ○ Dog sanitary facilities *(e.g. waste bins, bags)*
- ○ Dog showers
- ○ On-site dog walking area
- ○ Kennels
- ○ Vet nearby *(able to help with UK Pet Passports)*

Naturpark Schluga Seecamping

A-9620 Hermagor (Carinthia)
t: 042 822 051   e: camping@schluga.com
alanrogers.com/AU0450   www.schluga.com

Accommodation: ☑ Pitch ☑ Mobile home/chalet ○ Hotel/B&B ☑ Apartment

Facilities: Four heated modern toilet blocks are well constructed, with some washbasins in cabins and family washrooms for rent. Facilities for disabled campers. Washing machines and dryer. Motorcaravan services. Shop (20/5-10/9). Restaurant/bar by entrance and takeaway (all 20/5-10/9). Playground. Room for young people and children. Films. Kiosk and bar with terrace at beach. Surf school. Pedalo and canoe hire. Aqua jump and Iceberg. Pony rides. Bicycle hire. Weekly activity programme with mountain walks and climbs. Internet point. WiFi over site (charged). Off site: Fishing and sailing 200 m. Riding 12 km. Golf 16 km. Tennis.

Open: 10 May - 20 September.

Directions: Site is on B111 (Villach-Hermagor) 6 km. east of Hermagor town.

GPS: 46.63184, 13.44654

Charges guide

Per unit incl. 2 persons and electricity	€ 18,10 - € 33,75
extra person	€ 5,60 - € 8,85
child (5-14 yrs)	€ 4,00 - € 6,00
dog	€ 3,00 - € 3,90

This site is pleasantly situated on natural wooded hillside. It is about 300 m. from a small lake with clean water, where the site has a beach of coarse sand and a large grassy meadow where inflatable boats can be kept. There is also a small bar and a sunbathing area for naturists, although this is not a naturist site. The 250 pitches for touring units are on individual, level terraces, many with light shade and all with electricity (8-16A). One hundred and fifty-four pitches also have water, drainage and satellite TV and a further 47 pitches are occupied by a tour operator. This part of Carinthia is a little off the beaten track but the site still becomes full in season. Close by is Schluga Camping, under the same ownership, which is open all year. From both sites, there are views of the mountains, snowcapped in early summer. Many walks and attractive car drives are available in the area. English is spoken.

You might like to know

There are weekly mountain rambles for beginners, an ideal introduction to the mountains of the Gail valley or the Carnic ranges.

- ☑ Dogs welcome *(subject to conditions)*
- ☑ Dogs welcome all season
- ○ Dogs welcome part season
- ☑ Breed restrictions *(e.g. only small dogs accepted)*
- ☑ Number restrictions *(max. 1 or 2 dogs)*
- ○ Dog sanitary facilities *(e.g. waste bins, bags)*
- ○ Dog showers
- ○ On-site dog walking area
- ○ Kennels
- ☑ Vet nearby *(able to help with UK Pet Passports)*

Komfort-Campingpark Burgstaller

Seefeldstrasse 16, A-9873 Döbriach (Carinthia)
t: 042 467 774 e: info@burgstaller.co.at
alanrogers.com/AU0480 www.komfortcamping.at

Accommodation: ☑ Pitch ☑ Mobile home/chalet ○ Hotel/B&B ☑ Apartment

Facilities: Three exceptionally good quality toilet blocks include washbasins in cabins, facilities for children and disabled visitors, dishwashers and underfloor heating for cool weather. Seven private rooms for rent (3 with jacuzzi baths). Motorcaravan services. Bar. Good restaurant with terrace (May-Oct). Shop (May-Sept). Bowling alley. Disco (July/Aug). TV room. Sauna and solarium. Two play areas (one for under 6s, the other for 6-12 yrs). Bathing and boating on lake. Special entrance rate for lake attractions. Fishing. Bicycle hire. Mountain bike area. Riding. Comprehensive entertainment programmes. Covered stage and outdoor arena for church services (Protestant and Catholic, in German) and folk and modern music concerts. Off site: Mountain walks, climbing and farm visits all in local area.

Open: 12 April - 5 November.

Directions: Döbriach is at the eastern end of the Millstätter See, 15 km. southeast of Spittal. Leave A10 at exit 139 (Spittal, Millstätter) then proceed alongside northern shore of lake through Millstätter towards Döbriach. Just before Döbriach turn right and after 1 km. site is on left.

GPS: 46.77151, 13.64918

Charges guide

Per unit incl. 2 persons
and electricity € 19,10 - € 34,00

extra person € 7,00 - € 10,00

child (4-14 yrs) € 5,00 - € 8,00

dog € 3,00 - € 4,00

Discounts for retired people
in low season.

This is one of Austria's top sites in a beautiful location and with all the amenities you could want. You can always tell a true family run site by the attention to detail and this site oozes perfection. This is an excellent family site with a very friendly atmosphere, particularly in the restaurant in the evenings. Good English is spoken. The 590 pitches (540 for tourers) are on flat, well drained grass, backing onto hedges on either side of access roads. All fully serviced (including WiFi), they vary in size (45-120 sq.m) and there are special pitches for motorcaravans. One pitch actually rotates and follows the sun during the course of the day! The latest sanitary block warrants an architectural award; all toilets have a TV and a pirate ship on the first floor of the children's area sounds its guns every hour. The site entrance is directly opposite the park leading to the bathing lido, to which campers have free access. There is also a heated swimming pool. Much activity is organised here, including games and competitions for children and there are special Easter and autumn events.

You might like to know

The campsite is surrounded by the Carinthian Nockberge, which are perfect for mountain walking, whether you are an expert or a beginner.

- ☑ Dogs welcome *(subject to conditions)*
- ☑ Dogs welcome all season
- ○ Dogs welcome part season
- ☑ Breed restrictions *(e.g. only small dogs accepted)*
- ☑ Number restrictions *(max. 1 or 2 dogs)*
- ○ Dog sanitary facilities *(e.g. waste bins, bags)*
- ○ Dog showers
- ○ On-site dog walking area
- ○ Kennels
- ☑ Vet nearby *(able to help with UK Pet Passports)*

Facilities: Modern, bright, sanitary block is fully equipped including facilities for disabled visitors which double as a family shower room with a baby bath. Shop. Bar (1/5-1/10) with large screen for major sports events and films about the local flora/fauna. Takeaway food (July/Aug). Play area. Trampoline. Volleyball. Maps and walking routes are available from reception. WiFi (free in low season). Off site: Restaurant next door to site (all year). Restaurants, bars and shops in Ax-les-Thermes 7 km.

Open: All year.

Directions: From Ax-les-Thermes take D613 signed Quérigat, Quillan and Ascou-Pailhéres. After 3.6 km. turn right on D25 to site on right after 3.4 km.

GPS: 42.72444, 1.89274

Charges guide

Per unit incl. 2 persons
and electricity € 15,00 - € 22,00

extra person € 3,50 - € 5,50	
child (0-7 yrs) € 2,50 - € 3,50	
dog € 1,00 - € 1,50	

Credit cards accepted July/Aug. only.

France – Ascou

Camping Ascou la Forge

F-09110 Ascou (Ariège)
t: 05 61 64 60 03   e: info@ascou-la-forge.fr
alanrogers.com/FR09120   www.ascou-la-forge.fr

Accommodation: ☑ Pitch ☑ Mobile home/chalet ○ Hotel/B&B ☑ Apartment

The Dutch owners of Ascou la Forge will give you a warm, friendly welcome at their oasis in the mountains of the Pyrenees, close to the borders of Andorra and Spain. The site is 3,500 feet above sea level but is easily accessible for motorcaravans and caravans. Lying alongside the Lauze river, there are 50 grassy pitches, all with electricity (4-10A). There are also three chalets, two bungalows and one apartment available to rent. The site is quite open but a few trees scattered around provide some shade. The mountain views close to the site are outstanding and it is an ideal base for mountain walks and various outdoor sports. It is a perfect location for people who enjoy the tranquillity of the countryside although there is WiFi for those that must stay in touch. Social activities (at a small extra cost) are provided and include local wine and cheese evenings, pizza evenings, barbecues and picnics. The owners have a good knowledge of the local area and speak English.

You might like to know

Dogs are allowed on site and in rental accommodation. They can take a refreshing swim in the river and the reservoir. There are also many mountain lakes and rivers locally. Visitors with more than two dogs require permission.

☑ Dogs welcome *(subject to conditions)*
☑ Dogs welcome all season
○ Dogs welcome part season
○ Breed restrictions *(e.g. only small dogs accepted)*
☑ Number restrictions *(max. 1 or 2 dogs)*
○ Dog sanitary facilities *(e.g. waste bins, bags)*
○ Dog showers
☑ On-site dog walking area
○ Kennels
☑ Vet nearby *(able to help with UK Pet Passports)*

Campéole Clairefontaine

6 rue du Colonel Lachaud, F-17200 Royan-Pontaillac (Charente-Maritime)
t: 05 46 39 08 11 e: clairefontaine@campeole.com
alanrogers.com/FR17100 www.campeole.co.uk

Accommodation: ◉ Pitch ◉ Mobile home/chalet ○ Hotel/B&B ○ Apartment

Campéole Clairefontaine is situated on the outskirts of Royan, 300 m. from a golden sandy beach and a casino. This is a busy site which has benefited from much recent investment, and many of the facilities, especially the sanitary facilities, are of a high standard. There are 300 pitches, of which 115 are available for touring units. Electricity is available to all pitches, but some may require long leads. The site is mostly shaded and level with easy access to pitches. American motorhomes are accepted but care is needed on the entrance road to the site as it is not wide enough for two vehicles to pass. The reception area is large and welcoming and English is spoken. A programme of entertainment is provided in July and August and includes karaoke, singers and folk groups. There are many places of interest to visit, notably the nature reserves, the lighthouse at Cordouan, forests and the oyster beds of Marennes and Oléron.

Facilities: Two very modern sanitary blocks. Good facilities for disabled visitors. Washing machines. Ironing room. Motorcaravan services. Bar and restaurant with takeaway (June-mid Sept). Large swimming and paddling pools (from June). Four play areas. Games room with TV. Tennis. Basketball. Entertainment in high season. Internet access. WiFi in some areas (charged). Accommodation to rent (123 units). Off site: Beach and sailing 300 m. Bicycle hire 350 m. Fishing 200 m. Riding and golf 10 km.

Open: 6 April - 30 September.

Directions: Exit Royan on Avenue de Pontaillac towards La Palmyre. Turn right at the casino on the front, up Avenue Louise. Site is on left after 200 m. and is signed.

GPS: 45.631388, -1.050122

Charges guide

Per unit incl. 2 persons and electricity	€ 20,00 - € 31,70
extra person	€ 4,60 - € 9,60
child (2-10 yrs)	no charge - € 5,60
dog	€ 2,50 - € 3,50

You might like to know

Please note: a maximum of one dog per pitch (or mobile home) is allowed. Dogs must be kept on a lead on site.

- ◉ Dogs welcome *(subject to conditions)*
- ◉ Dogs welcome all season
- ○ Dogs welcome part season
- ◉ Breed restrictions *(e.g. only small dogs accepted)*
- ◉ Number restrictions *(max. 1 or 2 dogs)*
- ○ Dog sanitary facilities *(e.g. waste bins, bags)*
- ○ Dog showers
- ○ On-site dog walking area
- ○ Kennels
- ○ Vet nearby *(able to help with UK Pet Passports)*

Domaine de Soleil Plage

Caudon par Montfort, Vitrac, F-24200 Sarlat-la-Canéda (Dordogne)
t: 05 53 28 33 33 e: info@soleilplage.fr
alanrogers.com/FR24090 www.soleilplage.fr

Accommodation: ⦿ Pitch ⦿ Mobile home/chalet ○ Hotel/B&B ○ Apartment

This site is in one of the most attractive sections of the Dordogne valley, with a riverside location. There are 218 pitches, in three sections, with 119 for touring units. Additionally, there are 52 recently purchased mobile homes and 27 fully renovated chalets for rent. The site offers river swimming from a sizeable sandy bank or there is a very impressive heated pool complex. A covered, heated pool has been added. All pitches are bound by hedges and are of adequate size, 79 with 16A electricity, 45 also have water and a drain. Most pitches have some shade. If you like a holiday with lots going on, you will enjoy this site. Various activities are organised during high season including walks and sports tournaments, and daily canoe hire is available from the site. Once a week in July and August there is a 'soirée' (charged for) usually involving a barbecue or paella, with a band and some free wine – worth catching! The site is busy and reservation is advisable. You pay more for a riverside pitch, but these have fine river views. There is some tour operator presence.

Facilities: Toilet facilities are in three modern unisex blocks. One has been completely renovated to a high standard with heating and family shower rooms. Washing machines and dryer. Motorcaravan service point. Well stocked shop, pleasant bar with TV and attractive, newly refurbished restaurant with local menus and a pleasant terrace (all 7/5-14/9). Picnics available to order. Very impressive heated main pool, paddling pool, spa pool and two slides. Tennis. Minigolf. Three play areas. Fishing. Canoe and kayak hire. Bicycle hire. Currency exchange. Small library. WiFi throughout (charged). Activities and social events (high season). Max. 2 dogs. Off site: Golf 1 km. Riding 5 km. Many Dordogne attractions are within easy reach.

Open: 11 April - 29 September.

Directions: Site is 6 km. south of Sarlat. From A20 take exit 55 (Souillac) towards Sarlat. Follow the D703 to Carsac and on to Montfort. After Montfort castle site is signed on left. Continue for 2 km. down to the river and site.

GPS: 44.825, 1.25388

Charges guide

Per unit incl. 2 persons and electricity	€ 21,00 - € 36,60
incl. full services	€ 24,50 - € 52,00
extra person	€ 5,00 - € 7,70
child (2-8 yrs)	€ 3,00 - € 4,60
dog (max. 2)	€ 2,50 - € 3,50

You might like to know

The site is located at the heart of the Dordogne, alongside the Dordogne river, with some excellent walks close at hand.

- ⦿ Dogs welcome *(subject to conditions)*
- ⦿ Dogs welcome all season
- ○ Dogs welcome part season
- ⦿ Breed restrictions *(e.g. only small dogs accepted)*
- ⦿ Number restrictions *(max. 1 or 2 dogs)*
- ○ Dog sanitary facilities *(e.g. waste bins, bags)*
- ⦿ Dog showers
- ⦿ On-site dog walking area
- ○ Kennels
- ⦿ Vet nearby *(able to help with UK Pet Passports)*

Facilities: The toilet blocks are modern and heated in low season, with special facilities for disabled visitors. Shop (all season). Bar, snack bar and takeaway (limited in low season). Swimming pool. Fishing. Play area. Bicycle hire and riding. Entertainment and activity programme. Tents, Cahuttes and chalets for rent. Gas barbecues only. Max. 1 dog. Off site: Riding 4 km. Senonches (good selection of shops, bars and restaurants). Cycle and walking tracks. Chartres.

Open: 11 April - 4 November.

Directions: Approaching from Chartres, use the ring road (N154) and then take the D24 in a northwesterly direction. Drive through Digny and continue to Senonches, from where the site is well signed.

GPS: 48.5533, 1.04146

Charges guide

Per unit incl. 2 persons and electricity	€ 20,50 - € 38,10
extra person	€ 4,35 - € 6,40
child (2-7 yrs)	€ 2,75 - € 4,55
dog	€ 4,00

France – Senonches

Huttopia Senonches

Etang de Badouleau, avenue de Badouleau, F-28250 Senonches (Eure-et-Loir)
t: 02 37 37 81 40   e: senonches@huttopia.com
alanrogers.com/FR28140   www.huttopia.com

Accommodation: ☑ Pitch   ☑ Mobile home/chalet   ○ Hotel/B&B   ○ Apartment

Huttopia Senonches is hidden away in the huge Forêt Dominiale de Senonches, and in keeping with other Huttopia sites combines a high standard of comfort with a real sense of back-woods camping. There are 91 touring pitches here, some with 10A electricity. The pitches are very large, ranging from 100 sq.m. to no less than 300 sq.m. There are also 30 Canadian-style log cabins and tents available for rent. A good range of on-site amenities includes a shop and a bar/restaurant. The chlorine-free natural pool, with terrace, overlooks a lake and is open from early July until September. The forest can be explored on foot or by bicycle (hire available on site), and beyond the forest the great city of Chartres is easily visited; with its stunning Gothic cathedral it is widely considered to be the finest in France.

You might like to know

Senonches is located at the heart of a vast forest with an extensive network of footpaths. One dog is also accepted in the rental accommodation.

- ☑ Dogs welcome *(subject to conditions)*
- ☑ Dogs welcome all season
- ○ Dogs welcome part season
- ☑ Breed restrictions *(e.g. only small dogs accepted)*
- ○ Number restrictions *(max. 1 or 2 dogs)*
- ○ Dog sanitary facilities *(e.g. waste bins, bags)*
- ○ Dog showers
- ○ On-site dog walking area
- ○ Kennels
- ○ Vet nearby *(able to help with UK Pet Passports)*

France – Martres-Tolosane

Camping le Moulin

Lieu-dit le Moulin, F-31220 Martres-Tolosane (Haute-Garonne)
t: 05 61 98 86 40 e: info@campinglemoulin.com
alanrogers.com/FR31000 www.campinglemoulin.com

Accommodation: ☑ Pitch ☑ Mobile home/chalet ○ Hotel/B&B ○ Apartment

Facilities: Large sanitary block with separate ladies' and gents WCs. Communal area with showers and washbasins in cubicles. Separate heated area for disabled visitors with shower, WC and basin. Baby bath. Laundry facilities. Motorcaravan services. Outdoor bar with WiFi. Restaurant (1/7-20/8). Snack bar and takeaway (1/6-15/9). Daily bakers van (except Monday). Heated swimming and paddling pools (1/6-15/9). Fishing. Tennis. Canoeing. Archery. Walks in the countryside. BMX track. Playground. Games room. Bouncy castle. Entertainment programme and children's club (high season). Massage by arrangement (charged). Barbecues permitted. WiFi (in bar). Off site: Martres-Tolosane 1.5 km. Walking trails and cycle routes. Riding 4 km. Golf 12 km.

Open: 1 April - 30 September.

Directions: From the A64 motorway (Toulouse-Tarbes) take exit 21 (Boussens) or exit 22 (Martres-Tolosane) and follow signs to Martres-Tolosane. Site is well signed from village.

GPS: 43.19048, 1.01788

Charges guide

Per unit incl. 2 persons and electricity	€ 18,90 - € 27,90
extra person	€ 4,50 - € 6,00
child (under 7 yrs)	€ 2,50 - € 3,00
dog	€ 2,00 - € 2,50

Less 20% outside July/Aug.

With attractive, shaded pitches and many activities, this family run campsite has 12 hectares of woods and fields beside the River Garonne. It is close to Martres-Tolosane, an interesting medieval village. Some of the 60 level and grassy pitches are super-sized and all have electricity (6-10A). There are 17 chalets to rent. Summer brings opportunities for guided canoeing, archery and walking. A large sports field is available, with tennis, volleyball, basketball, boules and birdwatching on site. Facilities for visitors with disabilities are very good, although the sanitary block is a little dated. Some road noise. Large grounds for dog walking. Le Moulin is on the site of a 17th-century watermill, and the buildings have been traditionally restored. The friendly outdoor bar serves snacks and in summer the restaurant serves full meals. The swimming pool is large with an adjoining children's pool. During the high season, an organised activity and entertainment programme is on offer, including a children's club, karaoke, quiz and communal meal nights. A member of Sites et Paysages.

You might like to know

Dogs must be kept on a lead within the site. There is a large open space adjacent, along the banks of the Garonne (dogs can take a dip!), which is ideal for walking your dog.

- ☑ **Dogs welcome** *(subject to conditions)*
- ☑ **Dogs welcome all season**
- ○ **Dogs welcome part season**
- ○ **Breed restrictions** *(e.g. only small dogs accepted)*
- ☑ **Number restrictions** *(max. 1 or 2 dogs)*
- ☑ **Dog sanitary facilities** *(e.g. waste bins, bags)*
- ○ **Dog showers**
- ☑ **On-site dog walking area**
- ○ **Kennels**
- ☑ **Vet nearby** *(able to help with UK Pet Passports)*

Domaine du Logis

Le Logis, F-35190 La Chapelle-aux-Filtzmeens (Ille-et-Vilaine)
t: 02 99 45 25 45 e: domainedulogis@wanadoo.fr
alanrogers.com/FR35080 www.domainedulogis.com

Accommodation: ☑ Pitch ☑ Mobile home/chalet ○ Hotel/B&B ○ Apartment

This is an attractive rural site under new, young and enthusiastic ownership, set in the grounds of an old château. The site's upgraded modern facilities are housed in traditional converted barns and farm buildings, which are well maintained and equipped. There are a total of 188 pitches, 70 of which are for touring. The grass pitches are level, of a generous size and divided by mature hedges and trees. All have 10A electricity connections. This site would appeal to most age groups, with plenty to offer the active, including a new fitness room with a good range of modern equipment and a sauna for those who prefer to relax, or perhaps a quiet day's fishing by the lake. Although set in a quiet, rural part of the Brittany countryside, the nearby village of La Chapelle-aux-Filtzmeens has a bar, restaurant and shops. A 20 minute car ride will get you into the large town of Rennes, or perhaps travel north for 30 minutes to Mont Saint-Michel, Dinan, Dinard and the old fishing port of St Malo to sample the famous Brittany seafood.

You might like to know

The site staff can make appointments with the local vet on request.

- ☑ Dogs welcome *(subject to conditions)*
- ☑ Dogs welcome all season
- ○ Dogs welcome part season
- ☑ Breed restrictions *(e.g. only small dogs accepted)*
- ☑ Number restrictions *(max. 1 or 2 dogs)*
- ○ Dog sanitary facilities *(e.g. waste bins, bags)*
- ○ Dog showers
- ○ On-site dog walking area
- ○ Kennels
- ☑ Vet nearby *(able to help with UK Pet Passports)*

Facilities: One comfortable toilet block with washbasins and showers. Toilet and shower for disabled visitors. Laundry facilities. Bar with Sky TV (1/4-7/11). Restaurant and takeaway (1/7-29/8). Outdoor swimming pool (from 1/5). Fitness and games rooms. Sauna. BMX circuit. Bicycle hire. Unfenced play areas. Children's club (high season). Free WiFi. Lake fishing. Off site: Boating on the canal. Riding 10 km. Golf 15 km.

Open: 1 April - 7 November.

Directions: Turn south off N176 onto D795 signed Dol-de-Bretagne. Continue to Combourg then take D13 to La Chapelle-aux-Filtzmeens. Continue for 2 km. to site on right.

GPS: 48.37716, -1.83705

Charges guide

Per unit incl. 2 persons and electricity	€ 23,00 - € 30,00
extra person	€ 5,00 - € 5,50
child (2-12 yrs)	€ 2,50 - € 3,00
dog	€ 2,00

France – Villers-les-Nancy

Campéole le Brabois

Avenue Paul Muller, F-54600 Villers-les-Nancy (Meurthe-et-Moselle)
t: 03 83 27 18 28   e: brabois@campeole.com
alanrogers.com/FR54000   www.campeole.co.uk

Accommodation: ☑ Pitch ☑ Mobile home/chalet ○ Hotel/B&B ○ Apartment

Facilities: Four sanitary blocks have been completely updated. Facilities for babies and disabled visitors. Laundry facilities. Motorcaravan service point. Shop (incl. eggs and other produce grown on site). Bread to order. Restaurant with bar, takeaway and small shop (15/4-15/9). Library. Two playgrounds. WiFi (free from 2nd night). Off site: Restaurants, shops 1 km. Riding 1 km. Bicycle hire 2 km. Walking and cycling. Regular buses to Nancy.

Open: 1 April - 15 October.

Directions: From autoroute A33 take exit 2b for Brabois and continue for 500 m. to 'Quick' restaurant on left. Turn left, pass racetrack to T-junction, turn right and after 400 m. turn right on to site entrance road.

GPS: 48.66440, 6.14330

Charges guide

Per unit incl. 2 persons and electricity	€ 16,30 - € 19,80
extra person	€ 4,20 - € 6,00
child (2-6 yrs)	no charge - € 3,80
dog	€ 2,50 - € 2,70
hiker	€ 6,20 - € 8,80

Credit cards minimum € 15.
Barrier card deposit € 20.

This former municipal site is within the Nancy city boundary and 5 km. from the centre. Situated within a forest area, there is shade in most parts and, although the site is on a slight slope, the 174 good sized, numbered and separated pitches are level. Of these, 140 pitches have electrical connections (5/15A) and 10 also have water and drainage. Being on one of the main routes from Luxembourg to the south of France, le Brabois makes a good night stop. However, Nancy is a delightful city in the heart of Lorraine and well worth a longer stay. There are many attractions in the area including the interesting 18th-century Place Stanislas (pedestrianised) and 11th-century city centre. The British manager has a wide range of tourist literature, publishes a monthly English newsletter and is pleased to help plan visits and day trips. Horse racing takes place every two weeks at the Nancy race track next to the campsite, and good wine is produced nearby.

You might like to know

Dogs are welcome on the campsite, but must be kept on a lead.

- ☑ **Dogs welcome** *(subject to conditions)*
- ☑ **Dogs welcome all season**
- ○ Dogs welcome part season
- ☑ **Breed restrictions** *(e.g. only small dogs accepted)*
- ☑ **Number restrictions** *(max. 1 or 2 dogs)*
- ○ Dog sanitary facilities *(e.g. waste bins, bags)*
- ○ Dog showers
- ○ On-site dog walking area
- ○ Kennels
- ○ Vet nearby *(able to help with UK Pet Passports)*

Camping Indigo Royat

Route de Gravenoire, Quartier l'Oclède, F-63130 Royat (Puy-de-Dôme)
t: 04 73 35 97 05   e: royat@camping-indigo.com
alanrogers.com/FR63120   www.camping-indigo.com

Accommodation: ☑ Pitch   ☑ Mobile home/chalet   ○ Hotel/B&B   ○ Apartment

Facilities: Five well appointed toilet blocks, some heated. They have all the usual amenities but it could be a long walk from some pitches. Small shop (all season). Bar, restaurant and takeaway (July/Aug). Attractive heated swimming and paddling pools (26/4-16/9), sunbathing area. Tennis. Boules. Two grassy play areas. Organised entertainment in high season. Internet. Torches advised. Max. 1 dog. **Off site:** Royat 20 minutes walk. Bus service every 30 minutes in the mornings. Golf 7 km. Clermont-Ferrand, Puy-de-Dôme, Parc des Volcans and Vulcania Exhibition.

Open: 28 March - 4 November.

Directions: From A75 exit 2 (Clermont-Ferrand) follow signs for Bordeaux (D799). At third roundabout exit left signed Bordeaux. Shortly take exit right then turn right, signed Ceyrat. Leaving Ceyrat, at traffic lights take D941C signed Royat and Puy-de-Dôme. At top of hill turn left (D5) site signed. Entrance 800 m.

GPS: 45.7587, 3.05509

Charges guide

Per unit incl. 2 persons and electricity	€ 20,70 - € 29,80
extra person	€ 5,40 - € 6,10
child (2-7 yrs)	no charge - € 4,10
dog	€ 2,00 - € 4,00

This is a spacious and attractive site sitting high on a hillside on the outskirts of Clermont-Ferrand, but close to the beautiful Auvergne countryside. It has 197 terraced pitches on part hardstanding. There are 137 available for touring units, all with 10A electricity (long leads may be needed) and in addition five pitches offer water and drainage. The pitches are informally arranged in groups, with each group widely separated by attractive trees and shrubs. The bar and terrace overlooks the irregularly shaped swimming pool, paddling pool, sunbathing area, tennis courts and play areas. Although very peaceful off season, the site could be busy and lively in July and August. This site would be ideal for those who would like a taste of both the town and the countryside. Royat is a 20 minute walk, but a bus runs every 30 minutes in the mornings. Dotted with lakes and forests, the Auvergne has the greatest gathering of volcanoes in Europe. The unique European Volcano theme park, Vulcania, is less than twenty minutes away from the campsite.

You might like to know

This site is ideally located for exploring the mountainous region of the Massif Central, with its towering volcanoes. Discover the region's history at Parc Vulcania (less than 20 minutes by car).

- ☑ **Dogs welcome** *(subject to conditions)*
- ☑ **Dogs welcome all season**
- ○ **Dogs welcome part season**
- ○ **Breed restrictions** *(e.g. only small dogs accepted)*
- ☑ **Number restrictions** *(max. 1 or 2 dogs)*
- ○ **Dog sanitary facilities** *(e.g. waste bins, bags)*
- ○ **Dog showers**
- ○ **On-site dog walking area**
- ○ **Kennels**
- ○ **Vet nearby** *(able to help with UK Pet Passports)*

Camping Tamaris Plage

Quartier Acotz, 720 route des Plages, F-64500 Saint Jean-de-Luz (Pyrénées-Atlantiques)
t: 05 59 26 55 90   e: tamaris1@wanadoo.fr
alanrogers.com/FR64080   www.tamaris-plage.com

Accommodation: ☑ Pitch ☑ Mobile home/chalet ○ Hotel/B&B ○ Apartment

Facilities: The single heated toilet block of good quality and unusual design should be an ample provision. Facilities for disabled guests. Washing and drying machine. Wellness health club with free facilities: swimming pool, TV/playroom and club for children (4-11 yrs), and some on payment: gym, Turkish bath and other spa facilities, sunbathing area, jacuzzi, adult TV lounge. WiFi. Off site: Beach, fishing, surfing (with instruction) 30 m. Ghéthary with supermarket 2 km. St Jean-de-Luz 4 km. Bicycle hire, boat launching and golf 5 km. Riding 7 km.

Open: All year.

Directions: Proceed south on N10 and 1.5 km. after Ghéthary take first road on right (before access to the motorway and Carrefour centre commercial) and follow site signs.

GPS: 43.41795, -1.623817

Charges guide

Per unit incl. 2 persons and electricity	€ 18,00 - € 27,00
extra person (over 2 yrs)	€ 6,00 - € 8,00
dog	€ 6,00

This small, pleasant and popular site is well kept and open all year. It is situated outside the town and just across the road from a sandy beach. The 30 touring pitches, all with 7/10A electricity, are of a good size and separated by hedges, on slightly sloping ground with some shade. The site becomes full for July and August with families on long stays, so reservation then is essential. Mobile homes for rent occupy a further 40 pitches. A leisure centre and club provide a heated pool and various other free facilities for adults and children. A gym, Turkish bath, massage and other relaxing amenities are available at an extra charge. There is no shop, but bread is available daily across the road and some items can be bought in reception. Opposite the site, a popular surf school offers instruction to new and experienced surfers from the sandy Mayarco beach.

You might like to know

Spain is just 20 km. away – great for a day trip!

- ☑ Dogs welcome *(subject to conditions)*
- ☑ Dogs welcome all season
- ○ Dogs welcome part season
- ○ Breed restrictions *(e.g. only small dogs accepted)*
- ☑ Number restrictions *(max. 1 or 2 dogs)*
- ○ Dog sanitary facilities *(e.g. waste bins, bags)*
- ○ Dog showers
- ○ On-site dog walking area
- ○ Kennels
- ○ Vet nearby *(able to help with UK Pet Passports)*

DOUCHE CANIN[E]
RESERVEE AUX ANIMA[UX]

CANINE SHOWER
RESERVED FOR THE ANIMA[LS]

HUNDE DUSCHE
[R]ESERVIERTE FÜR DIE TIE[RE]

Facilities: Two toilet blocks, one behind reception, the other in the centre of the tent pitches. Traditional in style, they are bright and clean with modern fittings. Toilet for children and excellent facilities for disabled visitors. Shop (as site). Bar, restaurant and takeaway service (all July/Aug). Outdoor heated swimming pool (20/6-16/9). Washing machines and dryers at each block. Large games hall. Only electric barbecues are permitted. Max. 1 dog.
Off site: Bicycle hire 0.3 km. Golf and riding 2 km. Opportunities for walking and climbing are close by as are, fishing, cycling and tennis. The small town of Font-Romeu is very near with all the usual shops and banking facilities. Beach 8 km.

Open: 20 June - 16 September.

Directions: Font-Romeu is on the D118, some 12 km. after it branches off the N116 heading west, just after Mont Louis. This is an interesting road with magnificent views and well worth the climb. The site is just before the town, on the left and accessed off the car park.

GPS: 42.51171, 2.04972

Charges guide

Per unit with 2 persons and electricity	€ 21,00 - € 37,70
extra person	€ 5,40 - € 7,20
child (2-7 yrs)	€ 4,20 - € 4,90
dog	€ 2,50 - € 4,00

France – Font-Romeu

Huttopia Font-Romeu

Route de Mont-Louis, F-66120 Font-Romeu (Pyrénées-Orientales)
t: 04 68 30 09 32   e: font-romeu@huttopia.com
alanrogers.com/FR66250   www.huttopia.com

Accommodation: ☑ Pitch   ☑ Mobile home/chalet   ○ Hotel/B&B   ○ Apartment

This is a large, open site of some seven hectares, with 125 touring pitches (100 with 10A electricity), nestling on the side of the mountain at the entrance to Font-Romeu. This part of the Pyrenees offers some staggering views and the famous Mont Louis is close by. An ideal base for climbing, hiking and cycling, it would also provide a good stopover for a night or so whilst travelling between Spain and France, or to and from Andorra. The terraced pitches are easily accessed, with those dedicated to caravans and motorcaravans at the top of the site, whilst tents go on the lower slopes. Trees provide shade to many of the pitches from the sun, which can be quite hot at this altitude. Facilities on site are limited to very good toilet blocks and a very large games room and assembly hall, which is used by those in tents when it rains.

You might like to know

Font Romeu is one of France's oldest skiing resorts, and also home to the world's largest solar furnace!

- ☑ Dogs welcome *(subject to conditions)*
- ☑ Dogs welcome all season
- ○ Dogs welcome part season
- ○ Breed restrictions *(e.g. only small dogs accepted)*
- ☑ Number restrictions *(max. 1 or 2 dogs)*
- ○ Dog sanitary facilities *(e.g. waste bins, bags)*
- ○ Dog showers
- ○ On-site dog walking area
- ○ Kennels
- ○ Vet nearby *(able to help with UK Pet Passports)*

Facilities:
Large clean sanitary blocks include free hot showers and good facilities for disabled visitors. Laundry. Shop (1/5-15/9). Restaurant on site perimeter (closed Mon). Children's club (3/7-26/8) for 4-8 yrs. Safe deposit. WiFi (charged). Off site: Small supermarket adjacent to site. Good watersports area within 70 m. Access to town and beach from site. Fishing 100 m. Golf and riding 4 km. Bicycle hire 7 km.

Open: 30 May - 23 September.

Directions: Site is 16 km. south of Annecy on Route d'Albertville, well signed.

GPS: 45.7908, 6.2197

Charges guide

Per unit incl. 2 persons
and electricity € 17,50 - € 26,60

extra person € 4,50 - € 6,80

child (2-6 yrs) no charge - € 4,30

France – Doussard

Campéole la Nublière

30 allée de la Nublière, F-74210 Doussard (Haute-Savoie)
t: 04 50 44 33 44 e: nubliere@wanadoo.fr
alanrogers.com/FR74190 www.campeole.co.uk

Accommodation: ◉ Pitch ◉ Mobile home/chalet ○ Hotel/B&B ○ Apartment

If you are looking for large pitches, shady trees, mountain views and direct access to a lakeside beach, this site is for you. There are 271 touring pitches, of which 243 have electrical hook-ups (6A). This area is very popular and the site is very likely to be busy in high season. There may be some noise from the road and the public beach. La Nublière is 16 km. from old Annecy and you are spoilt for choice in how to get there. Take a ferry trip, hire a sailing boat or pedalo, or walk or cycle along the traffic free track towards the town. The local beach and sailing club are close and there is a good restaurant on the site perimeter. Across the road from the site are courts for tennis and boules. The site is perfect for walking, cycling or sailing and in low season provides a tranquil base for those just wishing to relax in natural surroundings on the edge of a nature reserve.

You might like to know

There are some great walks in the area. Dogs must be kept on a lead on site.

- ◉ Dogs welcome *(subject to conditions)*
- ◉ Dogs welcome all season
- ○ Dogs welcome part season
- ◉ Breed restrictions *(e.g. only small dogs accepted)*
- ◉ Number restrictions *(max. 1 or 2 dogs)*
- ○ Dog sanitary facilities *(e.g. waste bins, bags)*
- ○ Dog showers
- ○ On-site dog walking area
- ○ Kennels
- ○ Vet nearby *(able to help with UK Pet Passports)*

Campéole la Pinède

10 avenue de la plage, F-74140 Excenevex-Plage (Haute-Savoie)
t: 04 50 72 85 05   e: pinede@campeole.com
alanrogers.com/FR74280   www.campeole.co.uk

Accommodation: ⊘ Pitch ⊘ Mobile home/chalet ○ Hotel/B&B ○ Apartment

La Pinède is a member of the Campéole group and has direct access to Excenevex beach, the only naturally sandy beach on Lake Geneva. The site has a pleasant woodland setting and the 300 touring pitches are of a good size, all with 16A electricity. Mobile homes, chalets and fully equipped tents are available for rent (including specially adapted units for wheelchair users). There is a supervised bathing area on the beach, which shelves gradually, and a small harbour (suitable only for boats with a shallow draught). Other amenities include a shop and takeaway food service, as well as an entertainment marquee and children's play area. There is plenty of activity here in high season with a children's club and regular discos and karaoke evenings. Geneva is just 25 km. distant and other possible excursions include Thonon-les-Bains with its weekly market and, of course, boat trips on Lake Geneva. Dramatic mountain scenery is close at hand, notably the spectacular Dent d'Oche (2,222 m) and the Gorges du Pont du Diable.

You might like to know

The banks of Lake Geneva provide many opportunities for walking your dog. All dogs to be kept on a lead on the campsite.

- ⊘ Dogs welcome *(subject to conditions)*
- ⊘ Dogs welcome all season
- ○ Dogs welcome part season
- ⊘ Breed restrictions *(e.g. only small dogs accepted)*
- ⊘ Number restrictions *(max. 1 or 2 dogs)*
- ○ Dog sanitary facilities *(e.g. waste bins, bags)*
- ○ Dog showers
- ○ On-site dog walking area
- ○ Kennels
- ○ Vet nearby *(able to help with UK Pet Passports)*

Facilities: Heated toilet blocks include some private cabins, family shower room and facilities for children and disabled visitors. Washing machine. Motorcaravan service point. Lake beach. Fresh bread (July/Aug). Takeaway. Small swimming pool (15/6-10/9). Play area. Bouncy castle. Activities and entertainment programme. Bicycle hire. Tourist information. WiFi over part of site (charged). Mobile homes, chalets and equipped tents for rent. Off site: Hiking and cycle tracks. Riding 5 km. Golf 20 km. Thonon-les-Bains 15 km. Geneva 25 km.

Open: 12 April - 15 September.

Directions: From Geneva head along the south side of the lake on the D1005 as far as Massongy and shortly beyond here take the northbound D324 to Escenevex. The site is well indicated from here.

GPS: 46.34492, 6.35808

Charges guide

Per unit incl. 2 persons
and electricity € 17,10 - € 26,60

Camping Caravaning Esterel

Avenue des Golfs, Agay, F-83530 Saint Raphaël (Var)
t: 04 94 82 03 28 e: contact@esterel-caravaning.fr
alanrogers.com/FR83020 www.esterel-caravaning.co.uk

Accommodation: ☑ Pitch ☑ Mobile home/chalet ○ Hotel/B&B ○ Apartment

Facilities: Excellent refurbished, heated toilet blocks. Individual toilet units on 18 pitches. Facilities for disabled visitors. Laundry room. Motorcaravan services. Shop. Gift shop. Takeaway. Bar/restaurant. Five circular swimming pools (two heated), one for adults, one for children (covered and heated), three arranged as a waterfall (all season). Spa with sauna, etc. Disco. Archery. Minigolf. Tennis. Pony rides. Pétanque. Squash. Playground. Nursery. Bicycle hire. Organised events in season. No barbecues. Internet access. WiFi throughout. Baby club (3 months to 3 years). Off site: Golf nearby. Trekking by foot, bicycle or pony in l'Esterel forest park. Fishing and beach 3 km.

Open: 5 April - 27 September.

Directions: From A8, exit Fréjus, follow signs for Valescure, then for Agay, site is on left. The road from Agay is the easiest to follow but it is possible to approach from St Raphaël via Valescure. Look carefully for site sign, which is difficult to see.

GPS: 43.453775, 6.832817

Charges guide

Per unit incl. 2 persons and electricity	€ 18,00 - € 99,00
extra person	€ 9,00 - € 11,00
child (acc. to age)	€ 5,00 - € 10,00
dog	€ 4,00

Esterel is a quality, award-winning caravan site east of St Raphaël, set among the hills beyond Agay. The site is 3.5 km. from the sandy beach at Agay where parking is perhaps a little easier than at most places on this coast, but a shuttle runs from the site to and from the beach several times daily in July and August (€ 1). It has 164 touring pitches for caravans but not tents; all have 10A electricity and a water tap, 18 special ones have their own en-suite washroom adjoining whilst others also have a washing machine, a dishwasher, a jacuzzi, 16A electricity and free WiFi. Pitches are on shallow terraces, attractively landscaped with good shade and a variety of flowers, giving a feeling of spaciousness. Developed by the Laroche family for over 30 years, the site has an attractive, quiet situation with good views of the Esterel mountains. A pleasant courtyard area contains the shop and bar, with a terrace overlooking the beautifully landscaped (floodlit at night) pool complex. Great efforts have been made over the last year to improve the site's 'green credentials', including the planting of over 5,000 flowering shrubs in 2012.

You might like to know

There are some fine walks through the Esterel forest park – keep an eye out for the wild boar, though!

- ☑ Dogs welcome *(subject to conditions)*
- ☑ Dogs welcome all season
- ○ Dogs welcome part season
- ○ Breed restrictions *(e.g. only small dogs accepted)*
- ☑ Number restrictions *(max. 1 or 2 dogs)*
- ○ Dog sanitary facilities *(e.g. waste bins, bags)*
- ○ Dog showers
- ○ On-site dog walking area
- ○ Kennels
- ○ Vet nearby *(able to help with UK Pet Passports)*

Facilities: Private toilet blocks include a shower, washbasin and WC. Laundry area with washing machines. Very well stocked supermarket. Bar/restaurant with evening entertainment. Takeaway (all open all season). Large swimming pool complex with four water slides (all season). Two tennis courts. Sports area. Minigolf. Boules. Fishing. Bicycle hire. Kindergarten and Kid's Club. Play area. Nightclub (July/Aug). WiFi over site (charged). Only gas or electric barbecues are permitted. Off site: Riding 1.5 km. Golf 2 km. Saint Aygulf 2.5 km. Beach 4 km. Water skiing nearby.

Open: 31 March - 14 October.

Directions: Leave A8 at Le Muy exit 36 on N555 towards Draguignan then onto N7 towards Fréjus. Turn right on D7 signed Saint Aygulf and site is on right 2.5 km. before town.

GPS: 43.40905, 6.70893

Charges guide

Per unit incl. 2 persons and electricity € 25,00 - € 60,00	
extra person € 3,50 - € 7,00	
child (3-7 yrs) € 1,00 - € 5,00	
dog € 5,00	

Camping Résidence du Campeur

189 les Grands Chateaux de Villepey, RD 7, F-83370 Saint Aygulf (Var)
t: **04 94 81 01 59**   e: **residenceducampeur@sandaya.fr**
alanrogers.com/FR83050   www.sandaya.fr

Accommodation: ⦿ Pitch   ⦿ Mobile home/chalet   ○ Hotel/B&B   ○ Apartment

This excellent site near the Côte d'Azur will take you away from all the bustle of the Mediterranean coast. Spread out over ten hectares, this is a well equipped holiday destination with pitches arranged along avenues. The bar/restaurant is surrounded by a shady terrace, whilst friendly staff provide an excellent service. A pleasant pool complex is available for those who wish to stay on site instead of going swimming from the Mediterranean beaches. Saint Aygulf is 2.5 km. away, the nearest beach is 4 km. Activities are organised daily on the site during the summer season. The 136 touring pitches average 100 sq.m. in size and all have electricity connections and, unusually, private sanitary facilities (although washbasins double as dishwashing sinks). There are 238 accommodation units for rent, the majority of which were installed after significant investment by the owners, Sandaya, in 2012.

You might like to know

The site has an extensive aqua park yet is only 2.5 km. from the sandy beaches of the Côte d'Azur. Inland there are opportunities for rambling and mountain biking.

- ⦿ Dogs welcome *(subject to conditions)*
- ⦿ Dogs welcome all season
- ○ Dogs welcome part season
- ○ Breed restrictions *(e.g. only small dogs accepted)*
- ⦿ Number restrictions *(max. 1 or 2 dogs)*
- ○ Dog sanitary facilities *(e.g. waste bins, bags)*
- ○ Dog showers
- ○ On-site dog walking area
- ○ Kennels
- ○ Vet nearby *(able to help with UK Pet Passports)*

Camping les Pêcheurs

F-83520 Roquebrune-sur-Argens (Var)
t: 04 94 45 71 25 e: info@camping-les-pecheurs.com
alanrogers.com/FR83200 www.camping-les-pecheurs.com

Accommodation: ☑ Pitch ☑ Mobile home/chalet ○ Hotel/B&B ○ Apartment

Les Pêcheurs will appeal to families who appreciate natural surroundings with many activities, cultural and sporting. Interspersed with mobile homes, the 110 good sized touring pitches (10A electricity) are separated by trees or flowering bushes. The Provençal-style buildings are delightful, especially the bar, restaurant and games room with its terrace down to the river and the site's own canoe station (locked gate). Across the road is a lake with a sandy beach and restaurant. Enlarged spa facilities include a swimming pool, a large jacuzzi, massage, a steam pool and a sauna (some charges apply). Developed over three generations by the Simoncini family, this peaceful, friendly site is set in more than four hectares of mature, well shaded countryside at the foot of the Roquebrune Rock. Activities include climbing the Rock with a guide, trips to Monte Carlo, Ventimiglia (Italy) and the Gorges du Verdon, etc. The medieval village of Roquebrune is within walking distance.

You might like to know

Les Pêcheurs enjoys a natural setting beside a river and opposite a lake. Shady pitches are available; a maximum of one dog per pitch is allowed.

☑ Dogs welcome *(subject to conditions)*
☑ Dogs welcome all season
○ Dogs welcome part season
○ Breed restrictions *(e.g. only small dogs accepted)*
☑ Number restrictions *(max. 1 or 2 dogs)*
○ Dog sanitary facilities *(e.g. waste bins, bags)*
○ Dog showers
○ On-site dog walking area
○ Kennels
○ Vet nearby *(able to help with UK Pet Passports)*

Facilities: Modern, refurbished, well designed toilet blocks, baby baths, facilities for disabled visitors. Washing machines. Shop. Bar and restaurant (all open all season). Heated outdoor swimming pool (09.00-19.00, all season, lifeguard in high season, swim shorts not permitted), separate paddling pool, ice cream bar. Games room. Separate adults only pool and spa facilities. Playing field. Fishing. Minigolf. Miniclub (July/Aug). Activities for children and adults (high season), visits to local wine caves. Only electric barbecues allowed. WiFi throughout (charged). Security bracelets for all guests. Spring and late summer French courses (3 levels). Off site: Bicycle hire 1 km. Riding and golf 5 km. (reduced fees).

Open: 1 April - 30 September.

Directions: From A8 take Le Muy exit, follow N7 towards Fréjus for 13 km. bypassing Le Muy. After crossing A8, turn right at roundabout towards Roquebrune-sur-Argens. Site is on left after 1 km. just before bridge over river.

GPS: 43.450783, 6.6335

Charges guide

Per unit incl. 2 persons
and electricity € 23,00 - € 47,50

extra person	€ 4,00 - € 9,00
child (acc. to age)	no charge - € 6,80
dog (max. 1)	€ 3,20

Facilities: Six amenity blocks are well placed for all areas across the park. Facilities for disabled visitors. Family bathrooms and shower room. Hair dryers. Two launderettes. Gas available. Ice pack hire service. Bar (all year excl. Xmas and New Year). Shop (22/3-1/11). Fish and chip takeaway (22/3-5/10). Free outdoor swimming pool (24/5-14/9). Indoor pool (extra charge) open all year except Xmas and New Year. Arcade. Adventure playground, children's play areas and sports wall. Coarse fishing (from £5 per day). Caravan storage. Off site: Woodland walks and pub 0.5 miles. Beach 3 miles. Golf 3 miles. Riding 5 miles. Bicycle hire in Dawlish.

Open: All year.

Directions: Access to the park is off the A379 road 3 miles north of Dawlish, just after Cockwood Harbour village.
GPS: 50.6126, -3.460467

Charges guide

Per unit incl. 2 persons and electricity	£ 13,50 - £ 34,00
serviced pitch	£ 21,50 - £ 38,50
extra person (over 2 yrs)	£ 2,50 - £ 5,25
dog no charge - £ 5,25	

Small discount for senior citizens outside peak season.

Cofton Country Holidays

Starcross, Dawlish EX6 8RP (Devon)
t: 01626 890111   e: info@coftonholidays.co.uk
alanrogers.com/UK0970   www.coftonholidays.co.uk

Accommodation: ☑ Pitch ☑ Mobile home/chalet ○ Hotel/B&B ☑ Apartment

A popular and efficient family run park, Cofton is 1.5 miles from a sandy beach at Dawlish Warren. It has space for 450 touring units on a variety of fields and meadows with beautiful country views. Although not individually marked, there is never a feeling of overcrowding. The smaller, more mature fields, including a pleasant old orchard for tents only, are well terraced. While there are terraces on most of the slopes of the larger, more open fields, there are still some quite steep gradients to climb. There are some 450 electrical connections (10A), 30 hardstandings and 14 'super' pitches. Self-catering accommodation on site includes holiday homes, cottages and apartments. A well designed, central complex overlooking the pool and decorated with flowers and hanging baskets houses reception, a shop and off-licence and a traditional bar, the Cofton Swan. New for 2012 was an extension to this complex with another two bar areas suitable for daytime dining and evening entertainment, plus an indoor pool, sauna, steam room and gym, as well as a soft play area for children and a centrally located arcade.

You might like to know

There is a special dog walking area on site, as well as numerous walks in the surrounding countryside.

- ☑ Dogs welcome *(subject to conditions)*
- ☑ Dogs welcome all season
- ○ Dogs welcome part season
- ○ Breed restrictions *(e.g. only small dogs accepted)*
- ☑ Number restrictions *(max. 1 or 2 dogs)*
- ○ Dog sanitary facilities *(e.g. waste bins, bags)*
- ○ Dog showers
- ☑ On-site dog walking area
- ○ Kennels
- ○ Vet nearby *(able to help with UK Pet Passports)*

Wareham Forest Tourist Park

North Trigon, Wareham BH20 7NZ (Dorset)
t: 01929 551393   e: holiday@warehamforest.co.uk
alanrogers.com/UK2030   www.warehamforest.co.uk

Accommodation: ☑ Pitch ☑ Mobile home/chalet ○ Hotel/B&B ○ Apartment

This peacefully located and spacious park, on the edge of Wareham Forest, has 200 pitches and is continually being upgraded by its enthusiastic owners, Tony and Sarah Birch. The focal point of the park is the modern reception and shop, located by the pools. Four main areas provide a wide choice of touring pitches from grass to hardstanding and luxury, all with 16A electricity. Tent campers have a choice of open field or pinewood. The site has provided direct access for walkers into the forest or the seven miles of the Sika cycle trail may be used. The lovely market town of Wareham is accessible by bike without having to use the roads. This park has an almost continental feel, with plenty of space. Even when it is busy, it is calm and peaceful in its forest setting. In low season you may be lucky enough to spot the herd of Sika deer which live in the forest. The park is well situated to explore the Dorset coast and Thomas Hardy country. A member of the Best of British group.

Facilities: Two well maintained toilet blocks are of a good standard with some washbasins in cubicles, and several family bathrooms (one with baby bath). Main block was recently refurbished and both blocks are centrally heated. Facilities for disabled visitors. Well equipped laundry rooms. Motorcaravan service point. Small licensed shop with gas. Swimming pool (60x20 ft, heated 20/5-15/9). Large adventure play area. Barrier closed 23.00-07.00. Resident wardens on site. Caravan storage. WiFi. Off site: Cycle trail and walking in the forest. Bicycle hire and golf 3 miles. Fishing 5 miles. Riding 8 miles.

Open: All year.

Directions: From A31 Bere Regis, follow A35 towards Poole for 0.5 miles and turn right where signed to Wareham. Drive for a further 1.5 miles. First park on the left as you enter forest.
GPS: 50.721733, -2.156217

Charges guide

Per unit incl. 2 persons and electricity	£ 13,70 - £ 35,20
'superior' pitch fully serviced	£ 19,45 - £ 38,70
extra person	£ 3,10 - £ 5,60
child (5-15 yrs)	£ 2,00 - £ 3,90
dog	no charge - £ 1,75

Couples and families only.

You might like to know

A herd of Sika deer live in the forest – please take care when exercising your dog.

- ☑ Dogs welcome *(subject to conditions)*
- ☑ Dogs welcome all season
- ○ Dogs welcome part season
- ○ Breed restrictions *(e.g. only small dogs accepted)*
- ☑ Number restrictions *(max. 1 or 2 dogs)*
- ○ Dog sanitary facilities *(e.g. waste bins, bags)*
- ○ Dog showers
- ○ On-site dog walking area
- ○ Kennels
- ○ Vet nearby *(able to help with UK Pet Passports)*

Beacon Hill Touring Park

Blandford Road North, Poole BH16 6AB (Dorset)
t: **01202 631631** e: **bookings@beaconhilltouringpark.co.uk**
alanrogers.com/UK2180 www.beaconhilltouringpark.co.uk

Accommodation: ◉ Pitch ◉ Mobile home/chalet ○ Hotel/B&B ○ Apartment

Facilities: Two toilet blocks include facilities for disabled guests. Laundry facilities. Well stocked licensed shop at reception. Bar, takeaway and games room (19/7-1/9). Outdoor heated swimming pool (1/5-10/9). All weather tennis court (charged). Adventure play areas including a hideaway. TV room. WiFi (free). Two fishing lakes (on payment). Dog Walks. Off site: Bicycle hire 1 mile. Riding 2 miles. Poole harbour and ferries 3 miles. Golf 4 miles. Beach 8 miles. Brownsea Island, Studland beach with Sandbanks ferry and the Purbecks nearby.

Open: 18 March - 23 September.

Directions: Park is 3 miles north of Poole. Take A350 (towards Blandford) at roundabout where A350 joins A35. Park signed to the right (northeast) after 400 yds.
GPS: 50.74953, -2.03446

Charges guide

Per unit incl. 2 persons
and electricity £ 14,00 - £ 38,00

extra person £ 3,75 - £ 7,50

child (3-15 yrs) £ 2,50 - £ 4,00

dog £ 1,00 - £ 2,00

Beacon Hill is located in a marvellous, natural environment of partly wooded heathland, with areas of designated habitation for protected species such as sand lizards and the Dartford Warbler, but there is also easy access to main routes. Wildlife ponds encourage dragonflies and other species, but fishing is also possible. Conservation is obviously important in such a special area but one can ramble at will over the 30 acres, with the hilltop walk a must. Grassy open spaces provide 170 pitches, 151 with 10A electricity, on sandy grass. Of these, 50 are for tents only and a few are seasonal. The undulating nature of the land and trees allows for discrete areas to be allocated for varying needs, for example young families near the play area, families with teenagers close to the bar/games room, those with dogs near the dog walking area, and young people further away. The park provides a wide range of facilities, including an open-air swimming pool and a tennis court. It is well situated for beaches, Poole harbour and ferries for France and the Channel Isles.

You might like to know

The Park consists of 30 acres of beautiful, partly wooded heathland hosting an abundance of wildlife. Certain areas are designated Special Areas of Conservation.

◉ **Dogs welcome** (subject to conditions)
◉ **Dogs welcome all season**
○ **Dogs welcome part season**
○ **Breed restrictions** (e.g. only small dogs accepted)
◉ **Number restrictions** (max. 1 or 2 dogs)
○ **Dog sanitary facilities** (e.g. waste bins, bags)
○ **Dog showers**
○ **On-site dog walking area**
○ **Kennels**
○ **Vet nearby** (able to help with UK Pet Passports)

Facilities:
Good toilet facilities include some washbasins in cubicles for ladies, and an excellent en-suite room for disabled visitors. Laundry room. Shop (all essentials). Bar (evenings) and café with homemade and local food (open mornings, lunch and evenings, both with limited opening in low season). Packed lunches from reception. Special events monthly and games in main season. Hot tubs for hire, delivered to your pitch. Fly fishing lake. WiFi in some areas (charged). For rent on the park are B&B rooms, camping pods, lodges and yurts. Two lodges have been adapted for wheelchair users. Off site: Bicycle hire nearby. Riding 5 miles. Sailing and boat launching 8 miles. Golf 10 miles. Alton Towers 35 minutes drive. Go Ape. National Tramway Museum.

Open: 1 February - 5 January.

Directions: Park is 7 miles north of Ashbourne on the A515 to Buxton, on the eastern side of the road. It is well signed between the turnings east to Alsop Moor and Matlock (A5012), but take care as this is a fast section of the A515.

GPS: 53.106383, -1.760567

Charges guide

Per unit incl. 2 persons and electricity	£ 18,50 - £ 24,00
extra person	£ 2,50
child (4-15 yrs)	£ 2,00
dog	£ 2,00

Rivendale Caravan & Leisure Park

Buxton Road, Alsop-en-le-Dale, Ashbourne DE6 1QU (Derbyshire)
t: 01335 310311   e: enquiries@rivendalecaravanpark.co.uk
alanrogers.com/UK3850   www.rivendalecaravanpark.co.uk

Accommodation: ☑ Pitch ☑ Mobile home/chalet ☑ Hotel/B&B ○ Apartment

This unusual park has been developed in the bowl of a hill quarry which was last worked over 50 years ago. The steep quarry walls shelter three sides with marvellous views over the Peak District National Park countryside to the south. Near the entrance to the park is a renovated stone building which houses reception, a shop, a bar and a café/restaurant. Nearby are 136 level and landscaped pitches, mostly of a generous size with 16A electricity and a mix of hardstanding and grass. In two separate fields and a copse there is provision for 50 tents and that area includes a fishing lake. All the touring pitches are within easy reach of the central stone-built toilet block which is in keeping with the environment and provided with underfloor heating. A new lodge-style heated toilet block is at the entrance to the tent fields. For rent on the park are B&B rooms, camping pods, lodges and yurts. The park is almost on the Tissington Trail and links with the High Peak and Monsal Dale trails.

You might like to know

There is a network of footpaths directly accessible from the campsite, ideal for exercising dogs. Well behaved dogs are allowed in the bar.

☑ Dogs welcome *(subject to conditions)*
☑ Dogs welcome all season
○ Dogs welcome part season
○ Breed restrictions *(e.g. only small dogs accepted)*
☑ Number restrictions *(max. 1 or 2 dogs)*
○ Dog sanitary facilities *(e.g. waste bins, bags)*
○ Dog showers
○ On-site dog walking area
○ Kennels
○ Vet nearby *(able to help with UK Pet Passports)*

Riverside Caravan Park

High Bentham, Lancaster LA2 7FJ (North Yorkshire)
t: 01524 261272 e: info@riversidecaravanpark.co.uk
alanrogers.com/UK4715 www.riversidecaravanpark.co.uk

Accommodation: ✔ Pitch ✔ Mobile home/chalet ○ Hotel/B&B ✔ Apartment

The pretty, tree-lined approach to Riverside leads into an attractive park owned by the Marshall family for over 40 years. Nestling in beautiful countryside, alongside the River Wenning, the park has easy access to the Yorkshire Dales and the Lake District. There are 49 marked, level, grassy touring pitches with 16A electricity and TV hook-ups. In addition, there are 12 super pitches on tarmac. An area has been developed for 50 seasonal pitches on gravel. Located away from the touring area are 206 privately owned holiday homes. Tents are not accepted. The smart reception building includes a small shop selling caravan accessories. A new building opposite houses an excellent laundry and a library with Internet access and WiFi, a wide variety of books and local tourist literature. The Forest of Bowland is on the doorstep providing endless opportunities for walking and sightseeing in pretty villages. The small town of High Bentham is an easy walk from the park, and the local railway station links to the very scenic Settle to Carlisle railway. A member of the Best of British group.

You might like to know

Bentham has some lovely walks, ranging from a two-mile stroll along the river, to a ten-mile hike in the surrounding countryside.

- ✔ Dogs welcome *(subject to conditions)*
- ✔ Dogs welcome all season
- ○ Dogs welcome part season
- ✔ Breed restrictions *(e.g. only small dogs accepted)*
- ○ Number restrictions *(max. 1 or 2 dogs)*
- ○ Dog sanitary facilities *(e.g. waste bins, bags)*
- ○ Dog showers
- ○ On-site dog walking area
- ○ Kennels
- ○ Vet nearby *(able to help with UK Pet Passports)*

Facilities: The modern toilet block with underfloor heating is centrally situated. Washbasins in cubicles. Unisex showers in a separate area. Toilet and shower room for disabled visitors (Radar key). A new family shower/bathroom (charged). Motorcaravan services. Caravan storage. Outdoor play area for younger children. Large field for ball games. Family games room. The river can be used for fishing (permit from reception) swimming, and small boats. WiFi (charged). Off site: Golf and riding nearby.

Open: All year excl. 15-28 December.

Directions: Leave M6 at exit 34, and take the A683 towards Kirkby Lonsdale. After 5 miles take B6480 signed to High Bentham. From the east, take A65 after Settle. The site is signed at B6480, turn left. At Black Bull Hotel follow caravan signs. The park entrance is on right after crossing river bridge.

GPS: 54.11311, -2.51066

Charges guide

Per unit incl. 2 persons
and electricity £ 19,25 - £ 25,00

extra person £ 4,50

child (2-15 yrs) £ 2,50

dog £ 1,50

Min. charge per night £ 15,90.
Less 10% for bookings over 7 nights.

Facilities: New facilities were built in 2012 with underfloor heating, family rooms, drying rooms, laundry, and spacious showers. Small shop selling essentials and campers room with fridges and freezers. Fishing. Torches are useful. WiFi throughout. Off site: Pub at Hundred House village 1 mile. Bicycle hire and golf 5 miles. Riding 10 miles.

Open: March - January.

Directions: Park is 4 miles east of Builth Wells near the village of Hundred House on A481. Follow brown signs. Do not use postcode on sat nav.

GPS: 52.17121, -3.31621

Charges guide

Per unit incl. 2 persons and electricity £ 18,00	
extra person £ 3,00	
child (2-16 yrs) £ 3,00	
dog (max. 2) no charge	

Discounted low season rates for senior citizens. No credit cards.

Fforest Fields Caravan & Camping Park

Hundred House, Builth Wells LD1 5RT (Powys)
t: 01982 570406 e: office@fforestfields.co.uk
alanrogers.com/UK6320 www.fforestfields.co.uk

Accommodation: ☑ Pitch ☑ Mobile home/chalet ○ Hotel/B&B ○ Apartment

This secluded park is set on a family hill farm within seven acres in the heart of Radnorshire. This is simple country camping and caravanning at its best, with no clubhouse, swimming pool or games room. The facilities include 80 large pitches on level grass on a spacious and peaceful, carefully landscaped field by a stream. Electrical connections (mostly 16A) are available and there are 17 hardstanding pitches, also with electricity. Several additional areas without electricity are provided for tents. There are two new lakes, one for boating and fly fishing, the other for coarse fishing. George and Katie, the enthusiastic owners, have opened up much of the farm for ample woodland and moorland trails which can be enjoyed with much wildlife to see. Indeed, wildlife is actively encouraged with nesting boxes for owls, songbirds and bats, by leaving field margins wild to encourage small mammals and by annual tree planting.

You might like to know

This is a dog-friendly site and there are plenty of lovely farm and woodland walks direct from the site, making dog walking a real pleasure.

- ☑ Dogs welcome *(subject to conditions)*
- ☑ Dogs welcome all season
- ○ Dogs welcome part season
- ○ Breed restrictions *(e.g. only small dogs accepted)*
- ☑ Number restrictions *(max. 1 or 2 dogs)*
- ○ Dog sanitary facilities *(e.g. waste bins, bags)*
- ○ Dog showers
- ☑ On-site dog walking area
- ○ Kennels
- ○ Vet nearby *(able to help with UK Pet Passports)*

Brighouse Bay Holiday Park

Brighouse Bay, Borgue, Kirkcudbright DG6 4TS (Dumfries and Galloway)
t: 01557 870267 e: info@gillespie-leisure.co.uk
alanrogers.com/UK6950 www.brighouse-bay.co.uk

Accommodation: ☑ Pitch ☑ Mobile home/chalet ○ Hotel/B&B ☑ Apartment

Facilities: The large, well maintained main toilet block includes 10 unisex cabins with shower, basin and WC, and 12 with washbasin and WC. A second, excellent block next to the tent areas has en-suite shower rooms (one for disabled visitors) and bathroom, separate washing cubicles, showers and baby room. Laundry facilities. Motorcaravan service point. Gas supplies. Licensed shop. Bar, restaurant and takeaway (all year). Golf and Leisure Club with indoor pool (all year). Play area (incl. toddlers' area). Pony trekking. Quad bikes, boating pond, 10-pin bowling, playgrounds, putting. Nature trails. Coarse fishing ponds plus sea angling and an all-tide slipway for boating enthusiasts. Caravan storage. WiFi over site, free in bistro. Purpose built chalet for tourist information and leisure facility bookings. Off site: Small sandy beach nearby.

Open: All year.

Directions: In Kirkcudbright turn onto A755 and cross river bridge. In 400 yds. turn left onto B727 at international camping sign. Or follow Brighouse Bay signs off A75 just east of Gatehouse of Fleet.
GPS: 54.7875, -4.1291

Charges guide

Per unit incl. 2 persons
and electricity £ 19,50 - £ 26,00

extra person	£ 3,00
child (5-15 yrs)	£ 2,00
dog	£ 2,00

Contact park for full charges.
Golf packages in low season.

Hidden away within 1,200 exclusive acres, on a quiet, unspoilt peninsula, this spacious family park is only some 200 yards through bluebell woods from an open, sandy bay. It has exceptional all weather facilities, as well as golf and pony trekking. Over 90 percent of the 210 touring caravan pitches have 10/16A electricity, some with hardstanding and some with water, drainage and TV aerial. The three tent areas are on fairly flat, undulating ground and some pitches have electricity. There are 120 self-contained holiday caravans and lodges, of which about 30 are let, the rest privately owned. On-site leisure facilities include a golf and leisure club with 16.5 m. pool, water features, jacuzzi, steam room, fitness room, games room (all on payment), golf driving range, bowling green and clubhouse bar and bistro. The 18-hole golf course extends onto the headland with superb views over the Irish Sea to the Isle of Man and Cumbria. A nine-hole family golf course is a popular attraction. This is a well run park of high standards and a member of the Best of British group.

You might like to know

Brighouse Bay is surrounded by 1,200 acres of wonderful walking country.

- ☑ Dogs welcome *(subject to conditions)*
- ☑ Dogs welcome all season
- ○ Dogs welcome part season
- ○ Breed restrictions *(e.g. only small dogs accepted)*
- ☑ Number restrictions *(max. 1 or 2 dogs)*
- ○ Dog sanitary facilities *(e.g. waste bins, bags)*
- ○ Dog showers
- ☑ On-site dog walking area
- ○ Kennels
- ○ Vet nearby *(able to help with UK Pet Passports)*

Facilities:
New toilet and shower blocks. Next to the site is a range of amenities including a well stocked shop (open all year), a café serving a variety of meals and snacks, and a Forestry Commission visitor centre and souvenir shop. Barbecues are not permitted in dry weather. Bicycle hire. Fishing. Sandy beach (Blue Flag). Off site: The Aviemore centre with a wide range of indoor and outdoor recreation activities including skiing 7 miles. Golf within 15 miles. Fishing and boat trips.

Open: All year.

Directions: Immediately south of Aviemore on B9152 (not A9 bypass) take B970 then follow sign for Cairngorm and Loch Morlich. Site entrance is on right past the loch. If travelling in winter, prepare for snow.

GPS: 57.167033, -3.694717

Charges guide

Per unit incl. 2 persons	£ 14,50 - £ 30,00
incl. electricity	£ 19,50 - £ 35,00
extra person	£ 2,75 - £ 4,50
child (5-16 yrs)	£ 2,75 - £ 4,50

Discounts for families, disabled guests and senior citizens.

United Kingdom – Aviemore

Forest Holidays Glenmore

Aviemore PH22 1QU (Highland)
t: 01479 861271 e: info@forestholidays.co.uk
alanrogers.com/UK7680 www.campingintheforest.co.uk

Accommodation: ☑ Pitch ☑ Mobile home/chalet ○ Hotel/B&B ○ Apartment

Forest Holidays is a partnership between the Forestry Commission and The Camping and Caravanning Club. This site is attractively laid out in a fairly informal style in several adjoining areas connected by narrow, part gravel, part tarmac roads, with access to the lochside. One of these areas, the Pinewood Area, is very popular and has 32 hardstandings (some distance from the toilet block). Of the 220 marked pitches on fairly level, firm grass, 122 have 16A electricity. This site, with something for everyone, would be great for family holidays. The Glenmore Forest Park lies close to the sandy shore of Loch Morlich amidst conifer woods and surrounded on three sides by the impressive Cairngorm mountains. There is regular snowfall in the winter months. The park is conveniently situated for a range of activities, including skiing (extensive lift system), orienteering, hill and mountain walking (way-marked walks), fishing and non-motorised watersports on the Loch.

You might like to know

This site occupies an idyllic location beside the sandy beach at Loch Morlich in the Cairngorms National Park – you and your dog will enjoy the many great walks in the area.

- ☑ Dogs welcome *(subject to conditions)*
- ☑ Dogs welcome all season
- ○ Dogs welcome part season
- ○ Breed restrictions *(e.g. only small dogs accepted)*
- ☑ Number restrictions *(max. 1 or 2 dogs)*
- ○ Dog sanitary facilities *(e.g. waste bins, bags)*
- ○ Dog showers
- ○ On-site dog walking area
- ○ Kennels
- ○ Vet nearby *(able to help with UK Pet Passports)*

Facilities
The four modern toilet blocks with showers (extra showers in two blocks) and units for visitors with disabilities. An excellent block in Nevis Park (one of the eight camping fields) has some washbasins in cubicles, showers, further facilities for disabled visitors, a second large laundry room and dishwashing sinks. Motorcaravan service point. Shop (Easter-mid Oct), barbecue area and snack bar (May-mid Sept). Play area on bark. Off site: Fishing 1 mile. Golf 4 miles. Riding 4.5 miles.

Open: 15 March - 31 October.

Directions: Turn off A82 to east at roundabout just north of Fort William following camp sign.

GPS: 56.804517, -5.073917

Charges guide

Per unit incl. 2 persons
and electricity £ 16,50 - £ 22,50

extra person £ 1,80 - £ 3,20

child (5-15 yrs) £ 1,00 - £ 1,60

dog no charge

United Kingdom – Fort William

Glen Nevis Caravan & Camping Park

Glen Nevis, Fort William PH33 6SX (Highland)
t: 01397 702191 e: holidays@glen-nevis.co.uk
alanrogers.com/UK7830 www.glen-nevis.co.uk

Accommodation: ☑ Pitch ☑ Mobile home/chalet ◯ Hotel/B&B ☑ Apartment

Just outside Fort William, in a most attractive and quiet situation with views of Ben Nevis, this spacious park is used by those on active pursuits as well as sightseeing tourists. It comprises eight quite spacious fields, divided between caravans, motorcaravans and tents (steel pegs required). It is licensed for 250 touring caravans but with no specific tent limits. The large touring pitches, many with hardstanding, are marked with wooden fence dividers, 174 with 13A electricity and 100 also have water and drainage. The park becomes full in the peak months but there are vacancies each day. If reception is closed (possible in low season) you site yourself. There are regular security patrols at night in busy periods. The park's own modern restaurant and bar with good value bar meals is a short stroll from the park, open to all. A well managed park with bustling, but pleasing ambiance, watched over by Ben Nevis. Around 1,000 acres of the Glen Nevis estate are open to campers to see the wildlife and explore this lovely area.

You might like to know

The site is set in 34 acres of magnificent tree-clad countryside, which your dog will love exploring. There is no charge for dogs on the camping pitches.

- ☑ Dogs welcome *(subject to conditions)*
- ☑ Dogs welcome all season
- ◯ Dogs welcome part season
- ◯ Breed restrictions *(e.g. only small dogs accepted)*
- ☑ Number restrictions *(max. 1 or 2 dogs)*
- ◯ Dog sanitary facilities *(e.g. waste bins, bags)*
- ◯ Dog showers
- ◯ On-site dog walking area
- ◯ Kennels
- ◯ Vet nearby *(able to help with UK Pet Passports)*

Lough Ennell Camping & Caravan Park

Tudenham Shore, Mullingar (Co. Westmeath)
t: 044 934 8101 e: eamon@caravanparksireland.com
alanrogers.com/IR8965 www.caravanparksireland.com

Accommodation: ☑ Pitch ☑ Mobile home/chalet ○ Hotel/B&B ○ Apartment

Natural, rustic charm is the visitor's first impression on arrival at Lough Ennell Caravan Park. Set in 18 acres of mature woodland beside a Blue Flag lake, Eamon and Geraldine O'Malley run this sheltered and tranquil park with their family, who live on the site. They receive a blend of visitors – seasonal residents in camping holiday homes (private and to rent), caravanners and motorcaravanners and there are ample areas for tents. Pitches are varied, sheltered with trees and natural shrubbery, and with gravel or gravel and grass combinations. There are 44 touring pitches with electricity (7A Europlug) available on 25 hardstanding and grass pitches, with water points on or nearby all pitches; there are also 80 tent pitches. The site is a paradise for fishermen, with brown trout, rainbow trout, pike, tench, roach, perch, rudd and bream available. There is also one lake stocked with carp. Just an hour from Dublin, it provides a good holiday base or a useful stopover en-route to the West of Ireland. The watersports permitted on the lake include canoeing, sailing, windsurfing, boating, water skiing, fishing and safe swimming.

You might like to know

Dogs of restricted breeds are not accepted, and there are no exceptions to this rule. All dogs, no matter how small, must be on a lead at all times while on the campsite.

- ☑ Dogs welcome *(subject to conditions)*
- ☑ Dogs welcome all season
- ○ Dogs welcome part season
- ☑ Breed restrictions *(e.g. only small dogs accepted)*
- ○ Number restrictions *(max. 1 or 2 dogs)*
- ☑ Dog sanitary facilities *(e.g. waste bins, bags)*
- ○ Dog showers
- ☑ On-site dog walking area
- ○ Kennels
- ☑ Vet nearby *(able to help with UK Pet Passports)*

Facilities: The toilet block provides toilets, washbasins and hot showers (€1 coin). Additional dishwashing areas are around the park. Laundry. Small shop (all season). Café and coffee shop with takeaway. TV and games room. Play areas and area for ball games. Small lakeside beach. Fishing. Late arrivals area outside. Security including CCTV. Some breeds of dog are not accepted. Off site: Golf 1.5 km. Riding 4 km. Bicycle hire 6 km. Bus service 8 km. Boat hire on Lough Ennell and most other lakes.

Open: Easter/1 April - 30 September.

Directions: From N4 take the N52. Follow signs for Belvedere House and take turn 300 m. south of Belvedere House (signed for site). Continue to the shores of Lough Ennell and turn left. If in difficulty, telephone the site.

GPS: 53.466111, -7.375278

Charges guide

Per unit incl. 2 persons and electricity	€ 23,00 - € 25,00
extra person	€ 5,00
child	€ 3,00

No credit cards.

Blackwater Valley Caravan Park

Mallow-Killarney Road, Fermoy (Co. Cork)
t: 025 321 47 e: blackwatervalleycaravanpark@gmail.com
alanrogers.com/IR9470

Accommodation: ⦿ Pitch ⦿ Mobile home/chalet ◯ Hotel/B&B ◯ Apartment

Facilities: Modern, tiled toilet block provides the usual facilities including an en-suite shower room for disabled visitors. Laundry room with ironing facilities. Campers' kitchen with cooking facilities and dining area. TV and games room. Motorcaravan service point. Off site: Fishing adjacent to park. Internet access 100 m. Bicycle hire 1 km. Golf 3.5 km. Beach 35 km. Petrol station with gas across the road.

Open: 15 March - 31 October.

Directions: In Fermoy town take the N72 for Mallow. Park is 200 m. from the junction.

GPS: 52.141498, -8.281873

Charges guide

Per unit incl. 2 persons and electricity	€ 24,00
extra person	€ 6,00
child	€ 3,00

No credit cards.

The location of this park provides the best of both worlds, as it backs onto green fields adjacent to the Blackwater river, yet is within 200 metres of Fermoy town. Pat and Nora Ryan live overlooking the park which ensures supervision and prompt attention. Well situated for touring, there are 25 pitches, all with hardstanding and 13A electricity connections. Water taps are convenient to all pitches. Considerable additional space for tents is available towards the rear of the park. There are five caravan holiday homes to rent. Fermoy provides local amenities, such as a cinema, restaurants and pubs, many of these providing traditional music. The town park has a leisure centre with pool and an excellent play area is 100 metres on foot. The park owners also own the stretch of the Blackwater that is alongside – a huge plus for all campers who fancy trying their hand at fishing. A site suitable for motorcaravanners due to the proximity to the town centre. Many other attractions are within easy reach of the park.

You might like to know

This site can be found on the banks of the River Blackwater, just 200 metres from the town of Fermoy.

- ☑ Dogs welcome *(subject to conditions)*
- ☑ Dogs welcome all season
- ◯ Dogs welcome part season
- ◯ Breed restrictions *(e.g. only small dogs accepted)*
- ☑ Number restrictions *(max. 1 or 2 dogs)*
- ◯ Dog sanitary facilities *(e.g. waste bins, bags)*
- ◯ Dog showers
- ◯ On-site dog walking area
- ◯ Kennels
- ◯ Vet nearby *(able to help with UK Pet Passports)*

Facilities: Modern toilet facilities include showers on payment. En-suite unit for campers with disabilities. Laundry room. Campers' kitchen. Shop. Takeaway (8/7-25/8). TV lounge. Tennis. Play area. Picnic area. Games room. Security patrol. Off site: Fishing and golf 2 km. Riding 3 km. Bicycle hire 5 km. Woodland walk into Killarney. A visit to Killarney National Park is highly recommended.

Open: 1 April - 30 September.

Directions: Approaching Killarney from all directions, follow signs for N72 Ring of Kerry/Killorglin. At last roundabout join R562/N72. Continue for 5.5 km. and Fossa is the second park to the right.

GPS: 52.07071, -9.58573

Charges guide

Per unit incl. 2 persons and electricity € 22,00 - € 26,00	
extra person € 6,00	
child (under 16 yrs) € 2,50	
hiker/cyclist incl. tent € 8,00 - € 9,00	

Ireland – Killarney

Fossa Caravan & Camping Park

Fossa, Killarney (Co. Kerry)
t: 064 663 1497 e: fossaholidays@eircom.net
alanrogers.com/IR9590 www.fossacampingkillarney.com

Accommodation: ☑ Pitch ☑ Mobile home/chalet ○ Hotel/B&B ☑ Apartment

This park is in the village of Fossa, ten minutes by car or bus (six per day) from Killarney town centre. Fossa Caravan Park has a distinctive reception building and hostel accommodation, a stimulating play area and shop. The park is divided in two – the touring caravan area lies to the right, tucked behind the main building and to the left is an open grass area mainly for campers. Touring pitches, with 10/15A electricity and drainage, have hardstanding and are angled between shrubs and trees in a garden setting. To the rear at a higher level and discreetly placed are 30 caravan holiday homes, sheltered by the thick foliage of the wooded slopes which climb high behind the park. Not only is Fossa convenient for Killarney (5.5 km), it is also en-route for the famed Ring of Kerry, and makes an ideal base for walkers and golfers. Less than eight kilometres away are the famous walk up the Gap of Dunloe, and Carrantuohill, the highest mountain in Ireland.

You might like to know

Fossa Caravan & Camping Park is located on the Kerry Way. Killarney National Park, Gap of Dunloe, MacGillycuddy Reeks are all within easy distance of the site.

- ☑ Dogs welcome *(subject to conditions)*
- ☑ Dogs welcome all season
- ○ Dogs welcome part season
- ☑ Breed restrictions *(e.g. only small dogs accepted)*
- ☑ Number restrictions *(max. 1 or 2 dogs)*
- ○ Dog sanitary facilities *(e.g. waste bins, bags)*
- ○ Dog showers
- ○ On-site dog walking area
- ○ Kennels
- ☑ Vet nearby *(able to help with UK Pet Passports)*

Mannix Point Camping & Caravan Park

Cahirciveen (Co. Kerry)
t: 066 947 2806 e: mortimer@campinginkerry.com
alanrogers.com/IR9610 www.campinginkerry.com

Accommodation: ◉ Pitch ○ Mobile home/chalet ○ Hotel/B&B ○ Apartment

Facilities: Toilet and shower facilities were clean when we visited. Modern and well equipped campers' kitchen and dining area. Comfortable campers' sitting room. Laundry facilities with washing machines and dryer. Motorcaravan service point. Picnic and barbecue facilities. Fishing and boat launching from site. Off site: Bicycle hire 800 m. Riding 3 km. Golf 14 km. Pubs, restaurants and shops 15 minutes walk. Watersports, bird watching, walking and photography. Local cruises to Skelligs Rock with free transport to and from the port for walkers and cyclists.

Open: 15 March - 15 October.

Directions: Park is 300 m. off the N70 Ring of Kerry road, 800 m. southwest of Cahirciveen (or Cahersiveen) on the road towards Waterville.
GPS: 51.941517, -10.24465

Charges guide

Per unit incl. 2 persons and electricity	€ 27,00
extra person	€ 6,00

Reductions for activity groups and rallies if pre-paid. No credit cards.

A tranquil, beautifully located seashore park, it is no exaggeration to describe Mannix Point as a nature lovers' paradise. Situated in one of the most spectacular parts of the Ring of Kerry, overlooking the bay and Valentia Island, the rustic seven-acre park commands splendid views in all directions. The park road meanders through the level site and offers 42 pitches of various sizes and shapes, many with shelter and seclusion. There are 42 electrical connections (10A) available. A charming, old flower bedecked fisherman's cottage has been converted to provide facilities including reception, excellent campers' kitchen and a cosy sitting room with turf fire. There is no television, but compensation comes in the form of a knowledgeable, hospitable owner who is a Bord Fáilte registered local tour guide. A keen gardener, Mortimer Moriarty laid out the site over 20 years ago and his intention to cause as little disruption to nature as possible has succeeded. The site opens directly onto marshland which teems with wildlife (a two-acre nature reserve) with direct access to the beach and seashore.

You might like to know

Some excellent walking close to the site, including the Kerry Way.

- ☑ Dogs welcome *(subject to conditions)*
- ☑ Dogs welcome all season
- ☑ Dogs welcome part season
- ○ Breed restrictions *(e.g. only small dogs accepted)*
- ☑ Number restrictions *(max. 1 or 2 dogs)*
- ○ Dog sanitary facilities *(e.g. waste bins, bags)*
- ○ Dog showers
- ○ On-site dog walking area
- ○ Kennels
- ☑ Vet nearby *(able to help with UK Pet Passports)*

Fleming's White Bridge

Ballycasheen Road, Killarney (Co. Kerry)
t: 064 663 1590 e: info@killarneycamping.com
alanrogers.com/IR9620 www.killarneycamping.com

Accommodation: ☑ Pitch ☑ Mobile home/chalet ○ Hotel/B&B ○ Apartment

The main road from Cork to Killarney (N22) runs through the gentle valley of the River Flesk. Between the two sits Fleming's White Bridge camping park. Its ten-hectare site is within comfortable walking distance of Killarney centre. Surrounded by mature, broad-leafed trees, the park is flat, landscaped and generously adorned with flowers and shrubs. It comprises 92 pitches, the majority for touring caravans, on well kept grass pitches with electricity hook-ups, although some have concrete hardstanding and some pitches are reserved for tents. Well distributed around the park are three well appointed toilet blocks. This is obviously a site of which the owners are very proud. Hillary and Moira Fleming personally supervise the reception and grounds, maintaining high standards of hygiene, cleanliness and tidiness. In high season they even find time to organise on-site activities that keep children happy and parents relaxed. The park's location, so close to Ireland's premier tourism centre, makes it an ideal base to explore Killarney and the southwest.

You might like to know

Dogs are welcome here, but are not allowed in mobile homes.

- ☑ Dogs welcome *(subject to conditions)*
- ☑ Dogs welcome all season
- ○ Dogs welcome part season
- ○ Breed restrictions *(e.g. only small dogs accepted)*
- ☑ Number restrictions *(max. 1 or 2 dogs)*
- ○ Dog sanitary facilities *(e.g. waste bins, bags)*
- ○ Dog showers
- ○ On-site dog walking area
- ○ Kennels
- ○ Vet nearby *(able to help with UK Pet Passports)*

Facilities: Three toilet blocks are of a high standard. Motorcaravan service point. Campers' drying room and two laundries. Small shop (1/6-1/9). Two TV rooms and a games room. Fishing (advice and permits provided). Canoeing (own canoes). Bicycle hire. Woodland walks. Off site: Swimming pool and leisure centre 0.5 km. Kayaking 1.5 km. Golf 2 km. Riding and Killarney National Park 3 km.

Open: 15 March - 29 October.

Directions: From Cork and Mallow: at junction of N72/N22 continue towards Killarney and take first turn left (Ballycasheen Road). Proceed for 300 m. to archway entrance on left. From Limerick: follow N22 Cork road. Pass Super Valu and The Heights Hotel, take first right (signed Ballycasheen Road) and continue as above.

GPS: 52.05595, -9.47458

Charges guide

Per unit incl. 2 persons and electricity	€ 30,00
extra person	€ 8,00
child	€ 3,00

No credit cards.

Camping De Lilse Bergen

Strandweg 6, Gierle, B-2275 Lille (Antwerp)
t: 014 557 901   e: info@lilsebergen.be
alanrogers.com/BE0655   www.lilsebergen.be

Accommodation: ☑ Pitch   ☑ Mobile home/chalet   ○ Hotel/B&B   ○ Apartment

This attractive, quietly located holiday site has 513 shady pitches, of which 238 (all with 10A Europlug electricity) are for touring units. Set on sandy soil among pine trees and rhododendrons and arranged around a large lake, the site has a Mediterranean feel. It is well fenced, with a night guard and comprehensive, well labelled, fire-fighting equipment. Cars are parked away from units. The site is really child friendly with each access road labelled with a different animal symbol to enable children to find their own unit easily. An entertainment programme is organised in high season. The lake has marked swimming and diving areas (for adults), a sandy beach, an area for watersports, plus a separate children's pool complex (depth 50 cm) with a most imaginative playground. There are lifeguards and the water meets Blue Flag standards. A building by the lake houses changing rooms, extra toilets, showers and a baby room. There are picnic areas and lakeside and woodland walks.

Facilities: One of the six heated toilet blocks has been fully refitted to a good standard. Some washbasins in cubicles and good hot showers (on payment). Well equipped baby rooms. Facilities for disabled campers. Laundry. Barrier keys can be charged up with units for operating showers, washing machine etc. First aid post. Motorcaravan service point. Restaurant (all year, weekends only in winter), takeaway and well stocked shop (Easter-15/9; weekends only). Tennis. Minigolf. Boules. Climbing wall. Playground, trampolines and skateboard ramp. Pedaloes, kayaks and bicycles for hire. Children's electric cars and pedal kart tracks (charged for). Free WiFi over site.
Off site: Golf 1 km.

Open: All year.

Directions: From E34 Antwerp-Eindhoven take exit 22. On the roundabout take the exit for De Lilse Bergen and follow forest road to site entrance.
GPS: 51.28908, 4.85508

Charges guide

Per unit incl. 4 persons
and electricity € 20,00 - € 26,50

dog € 4,50

You might like to know

The lakeside and woodland walks are ideal for giving your dog a little exercise.

☑ Dogs welcome *(subject to conditions)*
☑ Dogs welcome all season
○ Dogs welcome part season
○ Breed restrictions *(e.g. only small dogs accepted)*
☑ Number restrictions *(max. 1 or 2 dogs)*
○ Dog sanitary facilities *(e.g. waste bins, bags)*
○ Dog showers
☑ On-site dog walking area
○ Kennels
☑ Vet nearby *(able to help with UK Pet Passports)*

Belgium – Oteppe

Camping l'Hirondelle

Rue de la Burdinale 76a, B-4210 Oteppe (Liège)
t: 085 711 131 e: info@lhirondelle.be
alanrogers.com/BE0705 www.lhirondelle.be

Accommodation: ☑ Pitch ☑ Mobile home/chalet ☑ Hotel/B&B ○ Apartment

This site is set in 20 hectares of woodland in the grounds of a castle that dates back to the 14th century. From the entrance one gets a glimpse of the restaurant in one part of the castle. There are 800 pitches with 300 for touring units, all with 6A electricity. The pitches are arranged around a huge playground, basketball court and a building housing a games room, a supermarket and a bar. In high season the site is bustling and lively, offering a full programme of entertainment with sports tournaments, discos and contests. This site has a lot to offer for families with children and teenagers. The large open-air pool (15x25 m) will accommodate all ages. A video circuit in all the buildings advertises and informs about the activity programmes.

You might like to know

L'Hirondelle is located within a national park, close to the villages of Huy, Andenne and Hannut, and with miles of excellent walking opportunities.

☑ Dogs welcome *(subject to conditions)*
☑ Dogs welcome all season
○ Dogs welcome part season
☑ Breed restrictions *(e.g. only small dogs accepted)*
☑ Number restrictions *(max. 1 or 2 dogs)*
○ Dog sanitary facilities *(e.g. waste bins, bags)*
○ Dog showers
☑ On-site dog walking area
○ Kennels
○ Vet nearby *(able to help with UK Pet Passports)*

Facilities: The two toilet blocks for touring units provide some washbasins in cabins, showers on payment, children's toilets and basins and a unisex baby room. Washing machine and dryer. Good provision for disabled visitors. These facilities will be very pressed to cope in high season. Shop. Bar. Restaurant. Swimming pool (15x25 m). Huge adventure type playground. Boules. Playing field. Entertainment (10/7-22/8). Games room. WiFi (free).

Open: 1 April - 31 October.

Directions: From Namen on the E42 take exit 10 towards Biewart then continue on the 80 to Burdinne. In Burdinne follow signs for Oteppe. The site is signed just before entering Oteppe.
GPS: 50.56758, 5.11718

Charges guide

Per unit incl. 2 persons
and electricity € 13,75 - € 21,00

extra person (over 3 yrs) € 2,75 - € 4,00

dog € 5,00

Ardennen Camping Bertrix

Route de Mortehan, B-6880 Bertrix (Luxembourg)
t: 061 412 281   e: info@campingbertrix.be
alanrogers.com/BE0711   www.campingbertrix.be

Accommodation: ☑ Pitch   ☑ Mobile home/chalet   ○ Hotel/B&B   ○ Apartment

Facilities: Five well appointed toilet blocks, one with facilities for disabled visitors. The central one has a large laundry. Motorcaravan service point. Shop for basics and bread. Excellent restaurant and bar (closed low season on Tues. and Thurs) has satellite TV and Internet access and a terrace overlooking the large, heated swimming and paddling pools (27/4-16/9, supervised high season). Tennis. Bicycle hire. Children's games room. Woodland adventure trail. Ardennes chalets and holiday homes for rent. WiFi in part of the site (charged). Max. 1 dog in July/Aug. Off site: Shops, banks, bars and restaurants in Bertrix 1.5 km. Canoeing. Fishing and boat launching 6 km. Riding 10 km. Walking and cycle trails.

Open: 28 March - 12 November.

Directions: Bertrix is 90 km. south of Namur. Take exit 25 from the E411 motorway and take N89 towards Bertrix. After 6.5 km. join the N884 to Bertrix then follow yellow signs to site south of town.
GPS: 49.83861, 5.25122

Charges guide

Per unit incl. 2 persons
and electricity € 20,00 - € 33,00

extra person (over 2 yrs) € 4,00 - € 5,50

dog € 4,00 - € 5,00

Bertrix is located at the heart of the Belgian Ardennes, between the towns of Bastogne and Bouillon and overlooking the hills of the Semois valley. Part of a Dutch chain, the site has 498 terraced pitches of which 303 are for touring, all with 10A electricity, and 43 also have water and drainage. A variety of seasonal caravans are sited among them and there is a friendly feel to the area. Some pitches are available with children's play huts on stilts! A wide range of imaginative activities are organised in the holidays, including some exciting excursions on horseback to the nearby working slate mine. There are many opportunities for walking, cycling and driving in the attractive countryside, with its wooded hills, valley and rivers, on which canoeing is popular. A trip to the nearby ruined castle at Bouillon is a must as well as experiencing the many Belgian beers. The war memorial and excellent museum at Bastogne commemorate the Battle of the Bulge. The town of Bertrix is unusual in its use of local slate not only on the roofs, but as cladding for the walls, and even the church spire.

You might like to know

A maximum of one pet is permitted per unit of rented accommodation.

- ☑ Dogs welcome *(subject to conditions)*
- ☑ Dogs welcome all season
- ○ Dogs welcome part season
- ○ Breed restrictions *(e.g. only small dogs accepted)*
- ☑ Number restrictions *(max. 1 or 2 dogs)*
- ○ Dog sanitary facilities *(e.g. waste bins, bags)*
- ○ Dog showers
- ○ On-site dog walking area
- ○ Kennels
- ○ Vet nearby *(able to help with UK Pet Passports)*

Panoramacamping Petite Suisse

Al Bounire 27, B-6960 Dochamps (Luxembourg)
t: 084 444 030   e: info@petitesuisse.be
alanrogers.com/BE0735   www.petitesuisse.be

Accommodation: ✓ Pitch ✓ Mobile home/chalet ○ Hotel/B&B ○ Apartment

This quiet site is set in the picturesque countryside of the Belgian Ardennes, a region in which rivers flow through valleys bordered by vast forests where horses are still usefully employed. Set on a southerly slope, the site is mostly open and offers wide views of the surrounding countryside. The 193 touring pitches, all with 10A electricity, are either on open sloping ground or in terraced rows with hedges in between, and trees providing some separation. Gravel roads provide access around the site. To the right of the entrance barrier a large wooden building houses reception, a bar and a restaurant. Close by is an attractive, heated outdoor swimming pool with wide terraces surrounded by grass. Behind this is a large play area adjoining a small terrace. Although the site has many activities on offer, the opportunity should not be missed to make excursions into the countryside with its hills and forests. The villages are filled with houses built from the local stone and small inviting bars and restaurants just waiting to be visited.

Facilities: All the facilities that one would expect of a large site are available. Showers are free, washbasins both open and in cabins. Baby room. Laundry room with washing machines and dryers. Shop, restaurant, bar and takeaway (2/4-5/11). Heated outdoor swimming pool (1/5-1/9), paddling pool and slide. Sports field. Tennis. Bicycle hire. Playground and club for children. Entertainment programme during school holidays. Varied activity programme, including archery, canoeing, climbing, abseiling and walking. WiFi (charged). Off site: La Roche en Ardennes and Baraque de Fraiture (ski resort) 10 km. Golf 20 km.

Open: All year.

Directions: From E25/A26 autoroute (Liège-Luxembourg) take exit 50 then the N89 southwest towards La Roche. After 8 km. turn right (north) on N841 to Dochamps where site is signed.
GPS: 50.23127, 5.62583

Charges guide

Per unit incl. 2 persons and electricity	€ 21,20 - € 42,20
extra person (over 4 yrs)	€ 4,25 - € 7,25
dog (high season max. 1)	€ 2,00 - € 5,00

You might like to know

La Petite Suisse is an ideal starting point for some fine walking, with nearby villages such as Dochamps and La Roche close at hand.

- ✓ Dogs welcome *(subject to conditions)*
- ○ Dogs welcome all season
- ✓ Dogs welcome part season
- ✓ Breed restrictions *(e.g. only small dogs accepted)*
- ✓ Number restrictions *(max. 1 or 2 dogs)*
- ○ Dog sanitary facilities *(e.g. waste bins, bags)*
- ○ Dog showers
- ○ On-site dog walking area
- ○ Kennels
- ✓ Vet nearby *(able to help with UK Pet Passports)*

Camping Floréal La Roche

Route de Houffalize 18, B-6980 La Roche-en-Ardenne (Luxembourg)
t: 084 219 467 e: camping.laroche@florealclub.be
alanrogers.com/BE0732 www.florealclub.be

Accommodation: ☑ Pitch ☑ Mobile home/chalet ○ Hotel/B&B ○ Apartment

Facilities: Six modern, well maintained sanitary blocks provide washbasins (open and in cabins), free preset showers. Facilities for disabled visitors. Baby room. Washing machines and dryers (token from reception). Motorcaravan service point. Well stocked shop (with fresh bread, pastries and newspapers in July/Aug). Bar, restaurant, snack bar and takeaway. At Camping Floréal 2: heated outdoor swimming pool. New wellness facilities with sauna and jacuzzi. Professional entertainment team (during local school holidays). Sports field. Volleyball. Tennis. Minigolf. Pétanque. Dog shower. WiFi. Mobile homes to rent. Off site: Mountain bike and canoe hire 300 m. Golf, riding and bicycle hire 1 km. Indoor pool 2 km. Skiing 15 km.

Open: All year.

Directions: From E25/A26 take exit 50 and follow N89 southwest to La Roche. In La Roche follow signs for Houffalize (beside Ourthe river). Floréal Club Camping 1 is 1.5 km. along this road. Note: go to camping 1 not 2.

GPS: 50.17600, 5.58600

Charges guide

Per unit incl. 2 persons
and electricity € 14,45 - € 22,85

extra person € 3,60	
child (3-11 yrs) € 2,60	
dog (max. 1) € 4,95	

Maintained to very high standards, this site is set in a beautiful wooded valley bordering the Ourthe river. Open all year, the site is located on the outskirts of the attractive small town of La Roche-en-Ardenne, in an area understandably popular with tourists. The site is large with 587 grass pitches (min. 100 sq.m), of which 290 are for touring units. The pitches are on level ground and all have 10/16A electricity and water connections. Amenities on site include a well stocked shop, a bar, a restaurant and takeaway food. In the woods and rivers close by, there are plenty of opportunities for walking, mountain biking, rafting and canoeing. For children there is a large adventure playground which is very popular and during the summer entertainment programmes are organised. The Ardennes region is rightly proud of its cuisine in which game, taken from the forests that cover the area, is prominent; for those who really enjoy eating, a visit to a small restaurant should be planned. English, French, Dutch and German are spoken in reception.

You might like to know

Pets are only admitted in Camping La Roche 1 (and not in the smaller, La Roche 2).

- ☑ Dogs welcome *(subject to conditions)*
- ☑ Dogs welcome all season
- ○ Dogs welcome part season
- ☑ Breed restrictions *(e.g. only small dogs accepted)*
- ☑ Number restrictions *(max. 1 or 2 dogs)*
- ○ Dog sanitary facilities *(e.g. waste bins, bags)*
- ☑ Dog showers
- ○ On-site dog walking area
- ○ Kennels
- ☑ Vet nearby *(able to help with UK Pet Passports)*

Facilities: New sanitary facilities include family bathrooms, baths with jacuzzi and jet stream (key access € 50 deposit). Provision for disabled visitors. Laundry facilities. Dog shower. Motorcaravan service point. Bar and snack bar. Tavern. Fishpond. Playground. Boules. Bicycle hire and free recharging of electric bikes. Free WiFi over site. No charcoal barbecues. Off site: Riding 6 km. Golf 10 km. Shops. Cycling and walking routes. National Park Hoge Kempen. Bobbejaanland. Maastricht. Hasselt. Genk.

Open: All year.

Directions: Take the Maaseik exit from the A2 (Eindhoven-Maastricht) motorway and drive via Neerpoeteren to Opoeteren. The site is on the right heading to Opglabbeek.

GPS: 51.0583, 5.6288

Charges guide

Per unit incl. 2 persons and electricity	€ 21,00 - € 30,00
extra person	€ 8,00
child (under 12 yrs)	€ 4,00
dog	€ 4,00

No credit cards.

Camping Zavelbos

Kattebeekstraat 1, B-3680 Opoeteren (Limburg)
t: 089 758 146 e: receptie@zavelbos.com
alanrogers.com/BE0792 www.zavelbos.com

Accommodation: ☑ Pitch ○ Mobile home/chalet ○ Hotel/B&B ☑ Apartment

Camping Zavelbos lies between woodland and moorland in a nature park of 2,000 hectares. It is a pleasant spot for nature lovers and those who love peace and quiet. There are many cycling and walking routes to enjoy in this beautiful region, alternatively you can simply relax in the peaceful campsite grounds complete with a large fishpond. There is no swimming pool but guests have free use of the pool complex at Wilhelm Tell Holiday Park (6 km). The 60 touring pitches (80-100 sq.m) all have 16A electricity (Europlug) and water. Bungalows and chalets are available to rent. The site is next to a wooded, hilly area, which has excellent off-road cycle and walking routes. Only five kilometres away is the Hoge Kempen National Park, covering almost 60 sq.km, and a haven for nature lovers. Guests receive a comprehensive welcome pack detailing the many local attractions. The site is open throughout the year and a children's club runs in high season.

You might like to know

In the immediate vicinity of Camping Zavelbos there is good access to walking routes throughout Kempen and Maasland.

☑ Dogs welcome *(subject to conditions)*
☑ Dogs welcome all season
○ Dogs welcome part season
☑ Breed restrictions *(e.g. only small dogs accepted)*
☑ Number restrictions *(max. 1 or 2 dogs)*
○ Dog sanitary facilities *(e.g. waste bins, bags)*
○ Dog showers
○ On-site dog walking area
○ Kennels
☑ Vet nearby *(able to help with UK Pet Passports)*

Facilities: Bar, restaurant and snack bar (all season). Swimming and paddling pools (15/5-1/9). Playground. Activities organised in high season. WiFi (free). Off site: Adventure park in village. 'Parc Merveilleux' funfair and Zoo, karting, bowling, National Mine Museum, preserved steam train. Fishing and bicycle hire 2 km. Golf 8 km. Riding 10 km. Arlon 10 km. Luxembourg 18 km.

Open: All year.

Directions: On A4/E25 from Belgium into Luxembourg, take first exit (no. 1) after the border. Follow signs to Steinfort (N4). Entrance to site is on the left just before the village (opposite petrol station).

GPS: 49.6583, 5.927

Charges guide

Per unit incl. 2 persons and electricity	€ 15,30 - € 23,00
extra person	€ 4,25 - € 5,00
child (2-10 yrs)	€ 3,40 - € 4,00
dog	€ 0,85 - € 1,00

Luxembourg – Steinfort

Camping Steinfort

72 rue de Luxembourg, L-8440 Steinfort (Luxembourg)
t: **398 827**   e: campstei@pt.lu
alanrogers.com/LU7720   www.camping-steinfort.lu

Accommodation: ☑ Pitch   ☑ Mobile home/chalet   ○ Hotel/B&B   ○ Apartment

Close to the Belgian border and convenient for the motorway route from Brussels to Luxembourg City, this could be useful for an overnight stay or for a longer visit to explore Luxembourg and southern Belgium. It is a pleasant site on the edge of the village of Steinfort with a choice of open or shady pitches and is open all year, as is its restaurant. Of the 142 pitches, 80 are for touring (all with electricity 16A and water), 4 units for hire and 56 private. The site becomes lively in high season, when numerous activities are organised. Walkers and cyclists can head straight out into the countryside and a fishing lake and an Adventure Park are nearby. The village centre is a short walk away and a neighbouring village has a good supermarket. For a wide range of shopping, cultural and leisure activities, the bustling city of Luxembourg is along the motorway to the east, whilst for a more relaxing outing the historic fortified town of Arlon is just across the border in Belgium.

You might like to know

For visitors in low season, the following formula applies: stays of 7 days = 6 days charged, 12=10, 14=11, 18=14 and 21=16. In high season (5/7-25/8), 1 child (2-10 yrs) per pitch stays free of charge. Offers only valid when booked in advance or on presentation of this printed offer.

- ☑ **Dogs welcome** *(subject to conditions)*
- ☑ **Dogs welcome all season**
- ○ **Dogs welcome part season**
- ○ **Breed restrictions** *(e.g. only small dogs accepted)*
- ○ **Number restrictions** *(max. 1 or 2 dogs)*
- ○ **Dog sanitary facilities** *(e.g. waste bins, bags)*
- ☑ **Dog showers**
- ☑ **On-site dog walking area**
- ○ **Kennels**
- ☑ **Vet nearby** *(able to help with UK Pet Passports)*

Camping Kautenbach

An der Weierbach, L-9663 Kautenbach (Luxembourg)
t: 950 303   e: info@campingkautenbach.lu
alanrogers.com/LU7830   www.campingkautenbach.lu

Accommodation: ☑ Pitch ☑ Mobile home/chalet ○ Hotel/B&B ○ Apartment

Facilities: Two toilet blocks with open style controllable washbasins and showers, baby changing. Facilities for disabled visitors (key). Laundry. Shop for basics (1/4-31/10, bread to order). Restaurant, bar/snack bar (all season). Direct river access. Fishing. Play area. Tourist information. Mobile homes for rent. Internet café. Off site: Walking and cycle trails. Railway station 500 m. Caves at Consdorf. Cathedral at Echternach.

Open: 20 January - 20 December.

Directions: Head south from Namur on A4, then join N4 (junction 15). Continue on N4 to Bastogne then join N84 towards Wiltz. Follow signs to Kautenbach on CR331 and site is well signed from here.

GPS: 49.95387, 6.0273

Charges guide

Per unit incl. 2 persons and electricity	€ 23,80 - € 25,35
extra person	€ 6,40
child (2-12 yrs)	€ 4,20
dog	€ 2,50

Kautenbach is situated in the heart of the Luxembourg Ardennes and was established over 50 years ago. Although in an idyllic location, it is less than a mile from a railway station with regular trains to Luxembourg city to the south. There are 135 touring pitches here, mostly of a good size and with reasonable shade. Most pitches have electrical connections (10A). This is excellent walking country with many tracks around the site. The site managers will be happy to recommend walks for all abilities. Kautenbach has an attractive bistro style restaurant, specialising in local cuisine, as well as a large selection of whiskies! The site has direct river access and fishing is popular (small charge applicable). During the high season, a wide range of activities are organised along with a lively children's club.

You might like to know

There are extensive walks for dogs and their owners.

☑ Dogs welcome *(subject to conditions)*
☑ Dogs welcome all season
○ Dogs welcome part season
○ Breed restrictions *(e.g. only small dogs accepted)*
☑ Number restrictions *(max. 1 or 2 dogs)*
☑ Dog sanitary facilities *(e.g. waste bins, bags)*
○ Dog showers
☑ On-site dog walking area
○ Kennels
☑ Vet nearby *(able to help with UK Pet Passports)*

Camping De Molenhoek

Molenweg 69a, NL-4493 NC Kamperland (Zeeland)
t: 0113 371 202   e: info@demolenhoek.com
alanrogers.com/NL5570   www.demolenhoek.com

Accommodation: ✔ Pitch   ✔ Mobile home/chalet   ○ Hotel/B&B   ○ Apartment

This rural, family run site makes a pleasant contrast to the livelier coastal sites in this popular holiday area. There is an emphasis on catering for the users of the 300 permanent or seasonal holiday caravans and 100 tourers. Eighty of these have 6A electricity, water and drainage. The site is neat and tidy with surrounding hedges and trees giving privacy and some shade, and electrical connections are available. A large outdoor pool area has ample space for swimming, children's play and sun loungers. Entertainment, including dance evenings and bingo, is organised in season. Although the site is quietly situated, there are many excursion possibilities in the area including the towns of Middelburg, Veere and Goes and the Delta Expo exhibition, which includes a waterpark, Neeltje Jans. It is close to Veerse Meer, which is very popular with watersports enthusiasts. The surrounding area has many beaches set among the dune landscape, and these are easily reached by car or bicycle.

Facilities: Two very clean and well appointed sanitary blocks include some washbasins in cabins and children's facilities. Toilet and shower facilities for disabled visitors and for babies. Laundry facilities. Motorcaravan services. Bar/restaurant with terrace and large TVs and LCD projection. Snack bar. Swimming pool (15/5-15/9). Playground. Bicycle hire. Pool tables. Sports field. Entertainment for children and teenagers. WiFi (charged). Off site: Tennis and watersports nearby. Riding 1 km. Shop 800 m. Fishing 2.5 km.

Open: 1 April - 27 October.

Directions: Site is west of the village of Kamperland on the island of Noord-Beveland. From the N256 Goes-Zierikzee road, exit west onto the N255 Kamperland road. Site is signed south of this road.

GPS: 51.57840, 3.69642

Charges guide

Per unit incl. 2 persons and electricity	€ 23,00 - € 36,00
extra person	€ 2,00 - € 3,50
dog	€ 4,00 - € 5,00

You might like to know

Noord-Beveland, the smallest island of the Province of Zeeland, has always resisted the temptation to change and offers some delightful walking opportunities. You and your dog are welcome at the nearest beach, 2.5 km. from the campsite.

- ✔ Dogs welcome *(subject to conditions)*
- ✔ Dogs welcome all season
- ○ Dogs welcome part season
- ○ Breed restrictions *(e.g. only small dogs accepted)*
- ✔ Number restrictions *(max. 1 or 2 dogs)*
- ✔ Dog sanitary facilities *(e.g. waste bins, bags)*
- ○ Dog showers
- ○ On-site dog walking area
- ○ Kennels
- ✔ Vet nearby *(able to help with UK Pet Passports)*

Camping De Veerhoeve

Veerweg 48, NL-4471 NC Wolphaartsdijk (Zeeland)
t: 0113 581 155   e: info@deveerhoeve.nl
alanrogers.com/NL5580   www.deveerhoeve.nl

Accommodation: ◉ Pitch ◉ Mobile home/chalet ○ Hotel/B&B ○ Apartment

Facilities: Sanitary facilities in three blocks have been well modernised with full tiling. Hot showers are on payment. Laundry facilities. Motorcaravan services. Supermarket. Restaurant and snack bar. TV room. Tennis. Playground and playing field. Games room. Bicycle hire. Fishing. Accommodation for groups. Max. 1 dog. WiFi (charged). Off site: Slipway for launching boats 100 m. Riding 2 km. Golf 5 km.

Open: 1 April - 30 October.

Directions: From N256 Goes-Zierikzee road take Wolphaartsdijk exit. Follow through village and signs to site (one site sign is obscured by other road signs and could be missed).

GPS: 51.54678, 3.81345

Charges guide

Per unit incl. up to 4 persons
and electricity € 20,00 - € 27,00

dog € 4,00

This is a family run site near the shores of the Veerse Meer, which is ideal for family holidays. It is situated in a popular area for watersports and is well suited for sailing, windsurfing and fishing enthusiasts, with boat launching 100 m. away. A sandy beach and recreation area, ideal for children, is only a five minute walk. As with most sites in this area there are many mature static and seasonal pitches. However, part of the friendly, relaxed site is reserved for touring units with 90 marked pitches on grassy ground, all with electrical connections. A member of the Holland Tulip Parcs group.

You might like to know

The Veerse Meer is a well known holiday area. Surfing, sailing, swimming and angling are all popular here. There are several woodland recreation areas nearby, which are ideal for a relaxing walk with your dog.

- ◉ Dogs welcome *(subject to conditions)*
- ◉ Dogs welcome all season
- ○ Dogs welcome part season
- ○ Breed restrictions *(e.g. only small dogs accepted)*
- ◉ Number restrictions *(max. 1 or 2 dogs)*
- ○ Dog sanitary facilities *(e.g. waste bins, bags)*
- ○ Dog showers
- ○ On-site dog walking area
- ○ Kennels
- ○ Vet nearby *(able to help with UK Pet Passports)*

Facilities: First class sanitary facilities are housed in five modern blocks that are clean, well maintained and well equipped. Good provision for babies and disabled guests. Laundry. Kitchen. Motorcaravan services. Gas supplies. Supermarket. Restaurant/bar. Lake beach and swimming. Fishing. Tennis. Minigolf. Boules. Five play areas. Bicycle hire. Organised activities. WiFi over site (charged). Off site: Riding 1 km. Golf 25 km.

Open: All year.

Directions: Leave A12 Utrecht-Arnhem motorway at Oosterbeek at exit 25 and join N310 to Otterlo. Then follow camping signs to site, watching carefully for entrance.

GPS: 52.09310, 5.77757

Charges guide

Per unit incl. 2 persons and electricity € 25,00 - € 38,00	
extra person € 8,00	
dog € 4,00	

Droompark De Zanding

Vijverlaan 1, NL-6731 CK Otterlo (Gelderland)
t: 0318 596 111   e: info@zanding.nl
alanrogers.com/NL5780   www.droomparkdezanding.nl

Accommodation: ☑ Pitch ☑ Mobile home/chalet ○ Hotel/B&B ○ Apartment

De Zanding is a highly rated, family run site that offers almost every recreational facility, either on site or nearby, that active families or couples might seek. As soon as you turn the corner to this impressive site, children will want to investigate the play equipment by the lake. There are many sporting options and organised high season programmes for all ages. There are 463 touring pitches spread around the site (all with 4/6/10A electricity), some individual and separated, others in more open spaces shaded by trees. Some serviced pitches are in small groups between long stay units and there is another area for tents. Seasonal units and mobile homes take a further 508 pitches. Minutes away is the Hoge Veluwe National Park, recommended for a great day out either cycling, walking or visiting the Kröller-Müller Museum (with the second largest collection of Van Gogh paintings after Amsterdam). In the village of Otterlo are a 14th-century Dutch Reformed Church and the Netherlands Tile Museum. A member of the Holland Tulip Parcs group.

You might like to know

Don't miss the Kröller-Müller museum, one of the world's finest collections of Van Gogh paintings.

- ☑ Dogs welcome *(subject to conditions)*
- ☑ Dogs welcome all season
- ○ Dogs welcome part season
- ○ Breed restrictions *(e.g. only small dogs accepted)*
- ☑ Number restrictions *(max. 1 or 2 dogs)*
- ○ Dog sanitary facilities *(e.g. waste bins, bags)*
- ○ Dog showers
- ○ On-site dog walking area
- ○ Kennels
- ○ Vet nearby *(able to help with UK Pet Passports)*

Facilities:
Three sanitary blocks include open style washbasins with cold water only, washbasins in cabins with hot and cold water, controllable showers (on payment). Family showers and baby bath. Facilities for disabled visitors. Cooking hob. Launderette. Motorcaravan services. Bar/restaurant (1/7-31/8). WiFi (charged). Play area. Bicycle hire. Boat launching. Pedalo and canoe hire. Fishing. Extensive entertainment programme (July/Aug). Bed and breakfast. Hikers' cabins and boarding houses. Dog exercise area. Off site: Beach 200 m. Riding 10 km.

Open: 1 April - 15 October.

Directions: From Leeuwarden take A31 southwest to Harlingen, then follow site signs.

GPS: 53.16237, 5.41688

Charges guide

Per unit incl. 2 persons and electricity	€ 22,30
extra person	€ 4,40
child (4-11 yrs)	€ 3,40
tent (no car) incl. 2 persons	€ 20,30
pet	€ 3,50

Netherlands – Harlingen

Camping De Zeehoeve

Westerzeedijk 45, NL-8862 PK Harlingen (Friesland)
t: 0517 413 465   e: info@zeehoeve.nl
alanrogers.com/NL6080   www.zeehoeve.nl

Accommodation: ☑ Pitch ☑ Mobile home/chalet ☑ Hotel/B&B ○ Apartment

Superbly located, directly behind the sea dyke of the Wadden Sea and just a kilometre from the harbour of Harlingen, De Zeehoeve is an attractive and spacious site. It has 300 pitches (125 for touring units), all with 16A electricity and 20 with water, drainage and electricity. There are 16 hardstandings for motorcaravans and larger units. Some pitches have views over the Harlingen canal where one can moor small boats. An ideal site for rest and relaxation, for watersports or to visit the attractions of Harlingen and Friesland. After a day of activity, one can wine and dine in the site restaurant or at one of the many pubs in the town. This splendid location allows one the opportunity to watch the sun slowly setting over the sea dyke. You can also stroll through Harlingen or take the ferry to Vlieland or Terschelling. It is possible to hire a boat or book an organised sailing or sea fishing trip from Harlingen.

You might like to know

This site is well placed for visiting the islands of Terschelling or Vlieland.

- ☑ Dogs welcome *(subject to conditions)*
- ☑ Dogs welcome all season
- ○ Dogs welcome part season
- ○ Breed restrictions *(e.g. only small dogs accepted)*
- ☑ Number restrictions *(max. 1 or 2 dogs)*
- ○ Dog sanitary facilities *(e.g. waste bins, bags)*
- ○ Dog showers
- ○ On-site dog walking area
- ○ Kennels
- ○ Vet nearby *(able to help with UK Pet Passports)*

Facilities:
Six neat, clean and heated toilet blocks (access by key; exclusively for campers). Washbasins in cabins, showers and family bathrooms (some charges for hot water). Laundry facilities. Well stocked supermarket, bar, restaurant and takeaway. Several play areas and children's farm. Watersports facilities and lake swimming. Fishing. Football pitch. Minigolf. Bicycle hire. Extended entertainment programme. WiFi (charged). Beach and shower for dogs. Off site: Golf 9 km. Riding 10 km.

Open: 28 March - 26 October.

Directions: From A28 (Utrecht-Zwolle) take exit 9 (Nijkerk/Almere) and follow N301 to Zeewolde. Cross the bridge and turn right following signs to site. From Amsterdam/Almere, take exit 5 and follow N27 (becomes N305) to Zeewolde. Then take N301 to Nijkerk. From bridge turn right and follow signs to site.

GPS: 52.27021, 5.48871

Charges guide

Per unit incl. 2 persons and electricity	€ 27,00
extra person	€ 3,25
dog	€ 2,00

Erkemederstrand Camping Horeca

Erkemederweg 79, NL-3896 LB Zeewolde (Flevoland)
t: 0365 228 421   e: info@erkemederstrand.nl
alanrogers.com/NL6200   www.erkemederstrand.nl

Accommodation: ◉ Pitch   ◉ Mobile home/chalet   ○ Hotel/B&B   ○ Apartment

Erkemederstrand is a leisure park in Flevoland with direct access to the Nuldernauw where there is a sandy beach, a lake and a forest. It provides a campsite for families, a marina, an area for youngsters to camp, a camping area for groups and a recreation area for day visitors. The campsite itself is divided into two areas: one before the dyke at the waterfront and one behind the dyke. The pitches are spacious (125-150 sq.m) and most have electricity, water and drainage. The focal point of the site and marina is the De Jutter beachside restaurant, offering a varied menu for more formal dining, as well as catering for snacks, takeaway, ice creams or a cold beer on the terrace. There is plenty to do on the campsite, including a Red Indian village where children can build huts, a children's farm and an extended programme of activities. The lake provides opportunities for watersports.

You might like to know

Dogs are more than welcome and allowed everywhere! There is a special 1.5 km. dog beach where they can run free and swim. The site has a dog shower, a dog sitter, a dog playground, free dog recreation programme (e.g. agility), and even drinking bowls in the restaurant!

- ☑ Dogs welcome *(subject to conditions)*
- ☑ Dogs welcome all season
- ○ Dogs welcome part season
- ○ Breed restrictions *(e.g. only small dogs accepted)*
- ○ Number restrictions *(max. 1 or 2 dogs)*
- ☑ Dog sanitary facilities *(e.g. waste bins, bags)*
- ☑ Dog showers
- ☑ On-site dog walking area
- ☑ Kennels
- ☑ Vet nearby *(able to help with UK Pet Passports)*

Facilities

Facilities: Modern sanitary facilities throughout. Private ensuite facilities to rent for some pitches. Children's sanitary block. Heated (1/5-15/9) outdoor adult and children's pools with sauna, water slide and solarium. Children's indoor play area. Shop, bar, restaurant. WiFi (charged). Bicycle hire. Tennis. Table tennis. Volleyball. Basketball. Terrace. Small animal park. Off site: Fishing 1 km. Riding 2 km. Golf 4 km. Running, cycling and walking tracks from site.

Open: All year.

Directions: Site is 60 km. east of Arnhem close to the border with Germany. From Winterswijk take A319 southeast for 2 km. then turn right onto De Slingeweg. Site is on outskirts of Winterswijk Brinkheurne.

GPS: 51.952137, 6.736899

Charges guide

Per unit incl. 2 persons and electricity	€ 18,00 - € 25,50
extra person	€ 3,25
dog	€ 3,00

Recreatiepark Het Winkel

De Slingeweg 20, NL-7115 AG Winterswijk (Gelderland)
t: 0543 513025   e: info@hetwinkel.nl
alanrogers.com/NL6412 www.hetwinkel.com

Accommodation: ☑ Pitch ☑ Mobile home/chalet ○ Hotel/B&B ☑ Apartment

Camping Het Winkel is a friendly family campsite in the middle of unspoilt countryside, surrounded by woodland in the Achterhoek region. The generous pitches have water and electricity plus there are caravans, chalets and studio apartments to rent. Some meadow areas (without electricity) are only for tents. There are large open spaces for leisure and sporting activities and a wide range of facilities for all the family. Cycling, running and walking routes start from the site. The Achterhoek region has the most extensive network of cycle paths in the Netherlands. There is a wide variety of sporting opportunities and in the high season there is an activity programme for children of all ages. There are many interesting places to visit nearby such as Erve Brookert which is a picturesque, historic building from 1875, originally a farmhouse, hayloft and klompenhuis where clogs were made, and now is open to the public, with a tea garden (limited opening).

You might like to know

Immediately adjacent to the park is a 3-hectare forest with a stream where you can walk the dog. You can also take a brisk walk on the large sand road network, directly accessible from the park.

- ☑ Dogs welcome *(subject to conditions)*
- ☑ Dogs welcome all season
- ○ Dogs welcome part season
- ○ Breed restrictions *(e.g. only small dogs accepted)*
- ☑ Number restrictions *(max. 1 or 2 dogs)*
- ○ Dog sanitary facilities *(e.g. waste bins, bags)*
- ○ Dog showers
- ☑ On-site dog walking area
- ○ Kennels
- ☑ Vet nearby *(able to help with UK Pet Passports)*

Netherlands – Hardenberg

Camping De Vechtvallei

Rheezerweg 76, NL-7795 DA Hardenberg (Overijssel)
t: 0523 25 18 00   e: info@devechtvallei.nl
alanrogers.com/NL6443   www.devechtvallei.nl

Accommodation: ☑ Pitch ☑ Mobile home/chalet ○ Hotel/B&B ○ Apartment

Facilities: Modern, heated sanitary facility with small toilets for children, baby bathroom. Restaurant and takeaway with terrace (all season). Swimming pool (heated 30/5-31/8). Small children's outdoor pool (May-Aug). Football and volleyball fields. Trampolines. Basketball. Holiday activity programme for all ages. Flower arranging workshop (on request). Internet café. Bicycle hire. WiFi throughout (charged). Off site: Hiking and cycle tracks nearby. River De Vecht for canoeing, boating, fishing 500 m. Rheezerweg 2.5 km. Hardenberg 7.5 km.

Open: 1 April - 31 October.

Directions: Camping De Vechtvallei is 6 km. southwest of Hardenberg. From A35 take exit 31 onto N36 for 22.7 km. then east onto Beerzerweg. After 350 m. turn left onto Stuwdijk and continue onto Rheezerweg. After 2.4 km. turn right onto restricted usage road and campsite is on right.

GPS: 52.535536, 6.569633

Charges guide

Per unit incl. 2 persons
and electricity € 15,00 - € 20,00

dog € 3,00

Camping De Vechtvallei is in the River Vecht valley, surrounded by a magnificent, varied scenery of forests, dunes and lakes. Of the 170 pitches, 45 are for touring, on grass and separated by hedges. Most have 10A electricity. There are central play areas for young children. In addition, there are chalets, hiker cabins and bungalows to rent. The countryside can be appreciated from the restaurant and bar terrace, and explored on foot and by bicycle on the many paths and tracks. Visitors can enjoy the sports and activities offered by the site that range from volleyball to flower arranging. The heated swimming pool with jacuzzi is open all year and the recreation programme which runs in holiday time caters for all ages. The restaurant serves snacks and a lunchtime menu as well as á la carte and is next to the bar which has a terrace that overlooks the countryside. There is an internet café. At the nearby De Vecht river, there is boating, canoeing and fishing and you can explore the river valley on the network of cycle paths. The owners of the site organise package deals (not July and Aug) based around a specific theme, for example, a fishing package.

You might like to know

Dogs are very welcome at our park as long as they are kept on a lead and walked off site. Just outside is a park with a pond, where you can take them for a walk and let them swim!

- ☑ **Dogs welcome** *(subject to conditions)*
- ☑ **Dogs welcome all season**
- ○ **Dogs welcome part season**
- ○ **Breed restrictions** *(e.g. only small dogs accepted)*
- ☑ **Number restrictions** *(max. 1 or 2 dogs)*
- ○ **Dog sanitary facilities** *(e.g. waste bins, bags)*
- ○ **Dog showers**
- ○ **On-site dog walking area**
- ○ **Kennels**
- ☑ **Vet nearby** *(able to help with UK Pet Passports)*

Facilities:
Facilities: Modern shower block. Play area. Bicycle hire. Tourist information. Off site: Amsterdam 20 km. Walking and cycle tracks. Golf. Beaches. WW2 museum.

Open: 1 April - 31 October.

Directions: Camping Schoonenberg is 20 km. northwest of Amsterdam. From A9 exit for Ijmuiden, follow signs towards Driehuis. On the way there are signs for Schoonenberg.

GPS: 52.45545, 4.64106

Charges guide

Per unit incl. 2 persons and electricity € 18,70	
extra person € 5,60	
child (0-12 yrs) € 4,40	
dog € 3,00	

Kampeerterrein Schoonenberg

Driehuizerkerkweg 15D, NL-1981 EH Velsen-Zuid (Noord-Holland)
t: 0255 52 39 98 e: info@campingschoonenberg.nl
alanrogers.com/NL6890 www.campingschoonenberg.nl

Accommodation: ☑ Pitch ○ Mobile home/chalet ○ Hotel/B&B ○ Apartment

Camping Schoonenberg is a family run campsite set in the heart of an oak forest. It is surrounded by 25 hectares of wooded estates. The campsite covers 2.5 hectares and is affiliated with the Nature Campgrounds organisation. The camping areas are car free except for loading; this makes it a very safe and friendly environment. Some of the 80 pitches have electricity connections, most have shade and are separated by mature bushes. The twice weekly evening bonfire is an ideal meeting place to make new friends and discuss the numerous activities nearby, many of which can be reached using hired bicycles. The surrounding area is full of nature related opportunities, from the uncommercialised North Sea beach at Ijmuiderslag to the animal and play park of Velserbeek. World War Two bunkers and museums tell the story of this land's recent history and its current importance. With three golf courses nearby and canoe hire in Spaarnwoude, this is the ideal location for a varied and interesting holiday.

You might like to know

Dogs on a lead are welcome on site. Off site they are free to explore the 25-hectare park nearby, or Ijmuiden beach (4 km) all year round.

- ☑ Dogs welcome *(subject to conditions)*
- ☑ Dogs welcome all season
- ○ Dogs welcome part season
- ○ Breed restrictions *(e.g. only small dogs accepted)*
- ○ Number restrictions *(max. 1 or 2 dogs)*
- ○ Dog sanitary facilities *(e.g. waste bins, bags)*
- ○ Dog showers
- ☑ On-site dog walking area
- ○ Kennels
- ○ Vet nearby *(able to help with UK Pet Passports)*

Strandpark De Zeeuwse Kust

Helleweg 8, NL-4326 LJ Noordwelle/Renesse (Zeeland)
t: 0111 468 282   e: info@strandparkdezeeuwsekust.nl
alanrogers.com/NL6948   www.strandparkdezeeuwsekust.nl

Accommodation: ☑ Pitch   ☑ Mobile home/chalet   ○ Hotel/B&B   ○ Apartment

Facilities: Modern, first class sanitary building providing showers, washbasins, private cabins, family shower rooms and other facilities for children and disabled visitors. Launderette. Shop/mini market. Fresh bread (all year). Heated swimming pool. Play areas (indoors and outdoors). Sports field. Motorcaravan service point. Outdoor table football. Games room with Xbox stations. Small film theatre. Recreation room. Entertainment team (special holidays, weekends and July-Aug). Sauna. Whirlpool. First aid post. Free WiFi. Dogs welcome all year – showers available near sanitary block. Off site: Riding 1 km. Fishing 5 km. Golf 7 km. Boat launching 8 km.

Open: All year (with most facilities).

Directions: From the A15 take exit 12 towards Middelburg. Follow the N57 through Ouddorp and then turn right on the N652. Immediately turn left for the N651 and follow to Noordwelle. Site is well signed.

GPS: 51.739062, 3.802369

Charges guide

Per unit incl. 2 persons, electricity, water and waste water	€ 20,00 - € 46,00
extra person (over 2 yrs)	€ 5,75
dog	€ 4,00

No credit cards.

Whether you want relaxation, something for the children, the seaside or activities, you will find all of these at De Zeeuwse Kust located just 250 m. from the sea with its beautiful sandy beach. The outstanding, hotel standard facilities contained within the centrally located building are in a class of their own, offering a haven whatever the weather. From the open-plan kitchen, the oversized wooden stools, to the open fireplace, they are all first class. This site has 168 spacious and comfortable pitches, some with private sanitary provision. The recreation team organises several activities for children all year. A heated pool and large indoor play area add to the facilities offered at this site which is highly recommended. There are walks and horse riding through the dunes, and the sea offers opportunities for kite surfing, diving, windsurfing and sailing (tuition available). This site is on the island of Schouwen-Duivenland, with views of the dunes and open countryside and just five minutes from the seaside resort of Renesse.

You might like to know

There are several dog exercise areas around the site, and a dog shower in the toilet block. They are also welcome on the beach.

- ☑ Dogs welcome *(subject to conditions)*
- ☑ Dogs welcome all season
- ○ Dogs welcome part season
- ○ Breed restrictions *(e.g. only small dogs accepted)*
- ○ Number restrictions *(max. 1 or 2 dogs)*
- ☑ Dog sanitary facilities *(e.g. waste bins, bags)*
- ☑ Dog showers
- ☑ On-site dog walking area
- ○ Kennels
- ☑ Vet nearby *(able to help with UK Pet Passports)*

Vikær Strand Camping

Dundelum 29, Diernæs, DK-6100 Haderslev (Sønderjylland)
t: 74 57 54 64   e: info@vikaercamp.dk
alanrogers.com/DK2022   www.vikaercamp.dk

Accommodation: ☑ Pitch ☑ Mobile home/chalet ○ Hotel/B&B ○ Apartment

Vikær Strand Camping in Southern Jutland lies in beautiful surroundings, right on the Diernæs Bugt beaches – ideal for both active campers and relaxation seekers. There are 390 grass pitches (210 for touring units), all with 10/16A electricity and separated by low hedges. Access is from long, gravel lanes. Forty newly developed, fully serviced pitches have electricity, water, drainage, TV aerial point and Internet. From these, and from the front pitches on the lower fields, there are marvellous views over the Diernæs Bugt. A Blue Flag beach runs along one edge of the site, and it can be narrow in places. It is well used for beach games, paddling and swimming. For the active, there are several routes for walking and cycling and, of course, sea fishing trips are possible. In the area are a newly developed swamp nature reserve, Schackenborg Castle and the battlefields of Dybbøl Banke.

You might like to know

There are some excellent coastal walks leading from the campsite.

- ☑ Dogs welcome *(subject to conditions)*
- ☑ Dogs welcome all season
- ○ Dogs welcome part season
- ☑ Breed restrictions *(e.g. only small dogs accepted)*
- ☑ Number restrictions *(max. 1 or 2 dogs)*
- ○ Dog sanitary facilities *(e.g. waste bins, bags)*
- ○ Dog showers
- ○ On-site dog walking area
- ○ Kennels
- ○ Vet nearby *(able to help with UK Pet Passports)*

Facilities: Three modern toilet blocks with washbasins in cabins and controllable hot showers. Family shower rooms. Children's section. Baby room. En-suite facilities for disabled visitors. Laundry. Campers' kitchen. Motorcaravan services. Shop (all season). Playground. Minigolf. Fishing. Archery. Watersports and boat launching. Pétanque. TV room. Play house with Lego and Play Station. Daily activities for children in high season. WiFi (charged). Torch useful. English is spoken. Off site: Riding 3 km. Golf 8 km. Bicycle hire 15 km.

Open: Week before Easter - 30 October.

Directions: From German/Danish border follow E45 north. Take exit 69 and follow to Hoptrup. From Hoptrup follow to Diernæs and Diernæs Strand.

GPS: 55.15029, 9.4969

Charges guide

Per person DKK 71	
child (under 12 yrs) DKK 47	
pitch DKK 41 - 72	
electricity DKK 35	
dog DKK 10	

Hampen Sø Camping

Hovedgaden 31, DK-7362 Hampen (Vejle)
t: 75 77 52 55 e: info@hampencamping.dk
alanrogers.com/DK2044 www.hampencamping.dk

Accommodation: ☑ Pitch ☑ Mobile home/chalet ○ Hotel/B&B ○ Apartment

Hampen Sø Camping is well placed for visits to Legoland, the Lion Park and Silkeborg. It is in a natural setting close to lakes and moors and there is good cycling and walking in this very pleasant area. There are 230 pitches in total, with 80 seasonal units plus 34 cabins. The pitches are arranged in large grassy bays taking around 15 units, and there are 10A electric hook-ups (long leads may be needed). Some aspects of this site, such as the free kitchens and a well stocked shop, are extremely good, and improvements are continuing. English is spoken by staff and they will be pleased to help you with tourist information and suggest itineraries. The nearby Hampen See lake is a pleasant walk through the forest and is said to be one of the cleanest swimming lakes in Denmark. The site is large and seems popular with visitors but there should always be space for touring units. There are 'camperstop' facilities for two motorcaravans to stay overnight outside the main site.

You might like to know

The site motto translates as 'camping as on a golf course' and regular checks on the ground ensure that the grass always looks its best.

☑ Dogs welcome *(subject to conditions)*
☑ Dogs welcome all season
○ Dogs welcome part season
○ Breed restrictions *(e.g. only small dogs accepted)*
☑ Number restrictions *(max. 1 or 2 dogs)*
○ Dog sanitary facilities *(e.g. waste bins, bags)*
○ Dog showers
○ On-site dog walking area
○ Kennels
○ Vet nearby *(able to help with UK Pet Passports)*

Facilities: Three toilet blocks, one basic near the entrance, one central on the site with new laundry, children's room and a kitchen, and one at the far end with two family shower rooms. En-suite facilities for disabled visitors. Laundry. Good supermarket. Bar, restaurant and takeaway (weekends only outside high season; restaurant open to the general public). Games and TV rooms. Very small outdoor pool (15/6-1/9). Covered minigolf. Trampolines and new play equipment. Race track for mini cars. WiFi (charged). Off site: Riding 500 m. Fishing 3 km. Golf and boat launching 10 km.

Open: All year.

Directions: Site is on road 176, 500 m. southwest of its junction with road 13 between Vejle and Viborg (50 km. south of Viborg). Look for Spar supermarket and camping signs. **GPS:** 56.01425, 9.36427

Charges guide

Per person DKK 72	
child (0-11 yrs) DKK 35	
electricity DKK 30	
dog DKK 10	

No credit cards.

Bøsøre Strand Feriepark

Bøsørevej 16, DK-5874 Hesselager (Fyn)
t: 62 25 11 45   e: info@bosore.dk
alanrogers.com/DK2210   www.bosore.dk

Accommodation: ◉ Pitch ◉ Mobile home/chalet ○ Hotel/B&B ○ Apartment

A themed holiday site on the eastern coast of Fyn, the tales of Hans Christian Andersen are evident in the design of the indoor pool complex, the minigolf course and the main outdoor play area. The former has two pools on different levels, two hot tubs, a sauna and features characters from the stories; the latter has a fairytale castle with a moat as its centrepiece. There are 300 pitches in total (some up to 150 sq.m), and with only 25 seasonal units there should always be room for touring units out of the main season. All have 10A electricity, there are 124 multi-serviced pitches and 20 hardstandings. In common with several other sites in Denmark, Bøsøre operates a card system which allows use of the facilities (showers, sauna, solarium, washing machine etc). You only pay for what you have used when you leave. The card also operates the barriers and opens doors to other facilities.

You might like to know

Occasional dog shows are organised in a special area of the site. For several years, these have included bulldogs, Bernese mountain dogs and schapendoes.

- ◉ Dogs welcome *(subject to conditions)*
- ◉ Dogs welcome all season
- ○ Dogs welcome part season
- ○ Breed restrictions *(e.g. only small dogs accepted)*
- ◉ Number restrictions *(max. 1 or 2 dogs)*
- ○ Dog sanitary facilities *(e.g. waste bins, bags)*
- ○ Dog showers
- ○ On-site dog walking area
- ○ Kennels
- ○ Vet nearby *(able to help with UK Pet Passports)*

Facilities: Sanitary facilities provide all the usual facilities plus some family bathrooms, special children's section, baby rooms and facilities for disabled visitors. They could be stretched in high season. Basic wellness facility. Laundry. Motorcaravan services. Shop, bar/restaurant, pizzeria, takeaway (all open all season). Kitchen (water charged). Solarium. Indoor pool complex. Games and TV rooms. Indoor playroom for toddlers. Playground with moat. Animal farm. Internet access and WiFi (charged). Bicycle hire. Entertainment (main season). Boat launching with jetty. Communal barbecue. Off site: Golf 10 km.

Open: Easter - 22 October.

Directions: Site is on the coast midway between Nyborg and Svendborg. From 163 road just north of Hesselager, turn towards coast signed Bøsøre Strand (5 km).
GPS: 55.19287, 10.80530

Charges guide

Per unit incl. 2 persons and electricity	DKK 214 - 274
extra person	DKK 79
child (0-11 yrs)	DKK 53 - 70
dog	DKK 20

Facilities:
Both sanitary buildings are equipped to high standards. Family bathrooms (with twin showers), complete suites for children and babies. Facilities for disabled visitors. Laundry. Kitchens, dining room and TV lounge. Excellent motorcaravan service point. Well stocked licensed shop. Licensed bistro and takeaway (1/5-20/10; weekends only outside peak season). Large, indoor swimming pool and paddling pool (charged). Minigolf. Games room. Indoor playroom and several playgrounds. Event camp for children. Pet zoo. Massage. Watersports. Fishing. WiFi. Off site: Abseiling and pool. Amusement park.

Open: All year.

Directions: From south on E47/55 take exit 38 towards Præsto. Turn north on 209 road towards Faxe and from Vindbyholt follow site signs. From the north on E47/55 take exit 37 east towards Faxe. Just before Faxe turn south on 209 road and from Vindbyholt, site signs.

GPS: 55.17497, 12.10203

Charges guide

Per unit incl. 2 persons and electricity DKK	265 - 340
extra person DKK	75
child (0-11 yrs) DKK	55
dog DKK	20

Denmark – Faxe

TopCamp Feddet

Feddet 12, DK-4640 Faxe (Sjælland)
t: 56 72 52 06   e: info@feddetcamping.dk
alanrogers.com/DK2255   www.feddetcamping.dk

Accommodation: ☑ Pitch ☑ Mobile home/chalet ○ Hotel/B&B ○ Apartment

This interesting, spacious site with ecological principles is located on the Baltic coast. It has a fine, white, sandy beach (Blue Flag) which runs the full length of one side, with the Præstø fjord on the opposite side of the peninsula. There are 413 pitches for touring units, generally on sandy grass, with mature pine trees giving adequate shade. All have 10A electricity and 20 are fully serviced. The sanitary buildings have been specially designed, clad with larch panels and insulated with flax mats. They have natural ventilation, controlled by sensors for heat, humidity and smell. Shaped blades on the roof increase ventilation on windy days. Heating, by a wood chip furnace (backed up by a rapeseed oil furnace), is CO_2 neutral and replaces 40,000 litres of heating oil annually. Rainwater is used for toilet flushing, but showers and basins are supplied from the normal mains, and urinals are water free. Water saving taps have an automatic turn off, and lighting is by low wattage bulbs with PIR switching. Recycling is very important here, with separate bins provided.

You might like to know

Dogs are allowed in a number of the campsite chalets.

- ☑ **Dogs welcome** *(subject to conditions)*
- ☑ **Dogs welcome all season**
- ○ **Dogs welcome part season**
- ○ **Breed restrictions** *(e.g. only small dogs accepted)*
- ☑ **Number restrictions** *(max. 1 or 2 dogs)*
- ○ **Dog sanitary facilities** *(e.g. waste bins, bags)*
- ○ **Dog showers**
- ○ **On-site dog walking area**
- ○ **Kennels**
- ○ **Vet nearby** *(able to help with UK Pet Passports)*

Facilities: Two modern and well decorated sanitary blocks with washbasins (some in cubicles), showers on payment, and toilets. Facilities for disabled visitors. Children's room. Laundry facilities. Kitchen. Motorcaravan services. Small shop, bar, restaurant and takeaway (all 1/5-30/9). TV room. Playground. Fishing. Motorboats, rowing boats, canoes, bicycles and pedal cars for hire. Bicycle hire. Go-kart sales. Free WiFi over site.
Off site: Cruises on the Sognefjord 400 m. The Norwegian Wild Salmon Centre 400 m. Riding 500 m. Golf 12 km. Skiing 20 km. The Flåm railway 40 km.

Open: All year,
by telephone request 1 Nov - 14 March.

Directions: Site is on road 5 (from the Oslo-Bergen road, E16) 400 m. north of Lærdal village centre.
GPS: 61.10037, 7.46986

Charges guide

Per unit incl. 2 persons and electricity	NOK 240
extra person	NOK 50
child (4-18 yrs)	NOK 25 - 37

Lærdal Ferie & Fritidspark

Grandavegens, N-6886 Lærdal (Sogn og Fjordane)
t: 57 66 66 95   e: info@laerdalferiepark.com
alanrogers.com/NO2375   www.laerdalferiepark.com

Accommodation: ☑ Pitch   ☑ Mobile home/chalet   ☑ Hotel/B&B   ☑ Apartment

This site is beside the famous Sognefjord, the longest fjord in the world. It is ideally situated if you want to explore the glaciers, fjords and waterfalls of the region. The 100 pitches are level with well trimmed grass, connected by tarmac roads and are suitable for tents, caravans and motorcaravans. There are 80 electrical hook-ups. The fully licensed restaurant serves traditional, locally-sourced meals as well as snacks and pizzas. The pretty little village of Lærdal, only 400 m. away, is well worth a visit. A walk among the old, small wooden houses is a pleasant and interesting experience. You can hire boats on the site for short trips on the fjord. Guided hiking, cycling and fishing trips are also available, with waymarked cycling and walking trails running through the park. Climbing excursions can be arranged on request. The site also provides 29 traditional Norwegian cabins, flats and rooms to rent, plus a motel, all very modern and extremely tastefully designed.

You might like to know

Dogs are welcome on site, but are not allowed in the chalets.

- ☑ **Dogs welcome** *(subject to conditions)*
- ☑ **Dogs welcome all season**
- ○ **Dogs welcome part season**
- ○ **Breed restrictions** *(e.g. only small dogs accepted)*
- ☑ **Number restrictions** *(max. 1 or 2 dogs)*
- ○ **Dog sanitary facilities** *(e.g. waste bins, bags)*
- ○ **Dog showers**
- ○ **On-site dog walking area**
- ○ **Kennels**
- ○ **Vet nearby** *(able to help with UK Pet Passports)*

Andenes Camping

Storgata 53, N-8483 Andenes (Nordland)
t: 76 14 14 12   e: camping@whalesafari.no
alanrogers.com/NO2428   www.andenescamping.no

Accommodation: ☑ Pitch   ○ Mobile home/chalet   ○ Hotel/B&B   ○ Apartment

Facilities: One building houses separate sex sanitary facilities, each providing two toilets, two showers (10 NOK) with curtain to keep clothes dry and three washbasins. In each, one toilet is suitable for disabled visitors and includes a washbasin. The reception building houses a well equipped kitchen, a large sitting/dining room, 2 showers, WC and washbasin. Laundry facilities. Motorcaravan service point. Chemical disposal (charged 30 NOK). Picnic tables. Swings for children. WiFi (free). Off site: Well stocked supermarket 250 m. On approach to town a garage, caravan dealer and another supermarket. From nearby village of Bleik (8 km), trips are available for deep sea fishing and to Bleiksøya, one of Norway's most famous bird cliffs with 80,000 pairs of puffins and 6,000 kittiwakes. Whalesafari 3 km. Guided walks. Kayaking.

Open: 1 June - 30 September.

Directions: Either take the scenic roads 946 and 947 on the west side of Andøy north or to the east road 82, site is on left 250 m. from where 947 rejoins the 82, 3 km. before Andenes. The scenic west route is 9 km. further.

GPS: 69.30411, 16.06641

Charges guide

Per pitch incl. electricity	NOK 200
tent pitch	NOK 100
car	NOK 100

Lying on the exposed west coast of Andøy between the quiet main road and white sandy beaches, this site has an exceptional location for the midnight sun. Extremely popular, offering mountain and ocean views, it is only three kilometres from the base of Whalesafari and Andenes town. There is space for an unspecified number of touring units and you park where you like. With only 20 places with 16A electricity connections, it is advisable to arrive by mid-afternoon. Late arrivals may pitch and pay later when reception opens. Level areas of grass with some hardstanding can be found on gently sloping ground. Visitors come to Andenes for the opportunities to see whales at close quarters. Whalesafari is deemed the world's largest, most successful Arctic whale watching operation for the general public. It has an over 90 per cent 'chance of seeing the quarry' and a 'whale guarantee' that offers a free second chance or your money back if your first trip fails to locate a whale. The nearby white sand beach, Bleikstranda, is the longest in the region.

You might like to know

Guided walks in the Forfjord countryside and the mountain of Forfjord. The oldest Norwegian pine is to be found here. Enjoy the magnificent view of Vesterålen.

- ☑ **Dogs welcome** *(subject to conditions)*
- ☑ **Dogs welcome all season**
- ○ **Dogs welcome part season**
- ☑ **Breed restrictions** *(e.g. only small dogs accepted)*
- ☑ **Number restrictions** *(max. 1 or 2 dogs)*
- ○ **Dog sanitary facilities** *(e.g. waste bins, bags)*
- ○ **Dog showers**
- ○ **On-site dog walking area**
- ○ **Kennels**
- ○ **Vet nearby** *(able to help with UK Pet Passports)*

Facilities:
Facilities: One heated toilet block provides washbasins, some in cubicles, and showers on payment. Family room with baby bath and changing mat, plus facilities for disabled visitors. Communal kitchen with cooking rings, small ovens, fridge and sinks (free hot water). Laundry facilities. Motorcaravan service point. Car wash facility. Barbecue area (covered). Playground. Duck pond. Fishing. Free WiFi over site. Old Trollveggen Station Master's appartment for hire by arrangement. Off site: Waymarked walks from site. Climbing, glacier walking and hiking. Fjord fishing. Sightseeing trips. The Troll Road. Mardalsfossen (waterfall). Geiranger and Åndalsnes.

Open: 10 May - 20 September.

Directions: Site is located on the E136 road, 10 km. south of Åndalsnes. It is signed.

GPS: 62.49444, 7.758333

Charges guide

Per unit incl. 2 persons and electricity	NOK 235
extra person (over 4 yrs)	NOK 15

Norway – Åndalsnes

Trollveggen Camping

Horgheimseidet, N-6300 Åndalsnes (Møre og Romsdal)
t: 71 22 37 00   e: post@trollveggen.no
alanrogers.com/NO2452   www.trollveggen.no

Accommodation: ◉ Pitch   ◉ Mobile home/chalet   ○ Hotel/B&B   ◉ Apartment

The location of this site provides a unique experience – it is set at the foot of the famous vertical cliff of Trollveggen (the Troll Wall), which is Europe's highest vertical mountain face. The site is pleasantly laid out in terraces with level grass pitches. The facility block, four cabins and reception are all very attractively built with grass roofs. Beside the river is an attractive barbecue area where barbecue parties are sometimes arranged. This site is a must for people who love nature. The site is surrounded by the Troll Peaks and the Romsdalshorn Mountains with the rapid river of Rauma flowing by. Here in the beautiful valley of Romsdalen you have the ideal starting point for trips to many outstanding attractions such as Trollstigen (The Troll Road) to Geiranger or to the Mardalsfossen waterfalls. In the mountains there are nature trails of various lengths and difficulties. The campsite owners are happy to help you with information. Åndalsnes is 10 km. away and has a long tourism tradition as a place to visit with its range of shops and restaurants.

You might like to know
There are great walking opportunities in the mountains surrounding the site and excellent hikes from the top of Trollstigen to the cliff face of Trollveggen. From here there are spectacular views of the Romsdal valley.

- ◉ Dogs welcome (subject to conditions)
- ◉ Dogs welcome all season
- ○ Dogs welcome part season
- ○ Breed restrictions (e.g. only small dogs accepted)
- ◉ Number restrictions (max. 1 or 2 dogs)
- ○ Dog sanitary facilities (e.g. waste bins, bags)
- ○ Dog showers
- ○ On-site dog walking area
- ○ Kennels
- ○ Vet nearby (able to help with UK Pet Passports)

Camping Havelberge am Woblitzsee

An den Havelbergen 1, Userin, D-17237 Gross Quassow (Mecklenburg-West Pomerania)
t: 039 812 4790 e: info@haveltourist.de
alanrogers.com/DE38200 www.haveltourist.de

Accommodation: ✓ Pitch ✓ Mobile home/chalet ○ Hotel/B&B ○ Apartment

The Müritz National Park is a very large area of lakes and marshes, popular for birdwatching as well as watersports, and Havelberge is a large, well equipped site to use as a base for enjoying the area. It is quite steep in places with many terraces, most with shade, and views over the lake. There are 400 pitches in total with 330 good sized, numbered touring pitches (all with 16A Europlug electrical connections) and 230 pitches on a newly developed area to the rear of the site with water and drainage. Pitches on the new field are level and separated by low hedges and bushes but have no shade. Over 330 seasonal pitches with a number of attractive chalets and an equal number of mobile homes in a separate area. In the high season this is a busy park with lots going on to entertain family members of all ages, whilst in the low seasons this is a peaceful base for exploring an unspoilt area of nature. A member of Leading Campings group.

You might like to know

There is a dog swimming area in the lake and waste bag stations on the site. Dogs can be walked on the site (on a lead) and in the forest. Agility training for dogs twice a week (April-October). Certain breeds are not accepted.

- ✓ Dogs welcome *(subject to conditions)*
- ✓ Dogs welcome all season
- ○ Dogs welcome part season
- ✓ Breed restrictions *(e.g. only small dogs accepted)*
- ✓ Number restrictions *(max. 1 or 2 dogs)*
- ✓ Dog sanitary facilities *(e.g. waste bins, bags)*
- ✓ Dog showers
- ✓ On-site dog walking area
- ○ Kennels
- ✓ Vet nearby *(able to help with UK Pet Passports)*

Facilities: Four sanitary buildings (one new and of a very high standard) provide very good facilities, with private cabins, showers on payment and large section for children. Fully equipped kitchen and laundry. Motorcaravan service point. Small shop, modern restaurant, bar, takeaway and wellness (all 1/4-31/10). The lake provides fishing, swimming from a small beach and boats can be launched (over 5 hp requires a German boat licence). Rowing boats, windsurfers and bikes can be hired. Canoe centre with beginners' courses and canoe hire. Accompanied canoe, cycle and walking tours. Play areas and entertainment for all the family in high season. Teepee vilage. Tree walkway (2.5 m. high with safety wires). WiFi (charged). Off site: Riding 1.5 km. (shuttle service from site).

Open: All year.

Directions: From A19 Rostock-Berlin road take exit 18 and follow B198 to Wesenberg and go left to Klein Quassow and follow site signs.

GPS: 53.30517, 13.00133

Charges guide

Per unit incl. 2 persons
and electricity € 26,60 - € 31,30

extra person	€ 4,40 - € 7,10
child (2-14 yrs)	€ 1,60 - € 4,70
dog	€ 1,00 - € 4,70

Camping & Ferienpark Teichmann

Zum Träumen 1A, D-34516 Vöhl-Herzhausen (Hessen)

t: 056 352 45   e: info@camping-teichmann.de

alanrogers.com/DE32800   www.camping-teichmann.de

Accommodation: ☑ Pitch ☑ Mobile home/chalet ○ Hotel/B&B ○ Apartment

Facilities: Three good quality sanitary blocks can be heated and have free showers, washbasins (open and in cabins), baby rooms and facilities for wheelchair users. Laundry. Motorcaravan services. Café and shop (both summer only). Restaurant by entrance open all day (closed Feb). Watersports. Boat and bicycle hire. Lake swimming. Fishing. Minigolf. Playground. Sauna. Solarium. Disco (high season). Internet access. Off site: New national park opposite site entrance. Riding 500 m. Golf 25 km. Cable car (bicycles accepted). Aquapark. Boat trips on the Edersee.

Open: All year.

Directions: Site is 45 km. southwest of Kassel. From A44 Oberhausen-Kassel autobahn, take exit 64 for Diemelstadt and head south for Korbach. Site is between Korbach and Frankenberg on the B252 road, 1 km. to the south of Herzhausen at pedestrian traffic lights.

GPS: 51.17550, 8.89067

Charges guide

Per unit incl. 2 persons and electricity	€ 26,00 - € 30,50
extra person	€ 5,90 - € 7,50
child (3-15 yrs)	€ 3,50 - € 4,40
dog	€ 3,60

Situated near the eastern end of the 27 km. long Edersee and the Kellerwald-Edersee National Park, this attractively set site is surrounded by wooded hills and encircles a six-hectare lake, which has separate areas for swimming, fishing and boating. Of the 500 pitches, 250 are for touring; all have 10A electricity and 50 have fresh and waste water connections. The pitches are on level grass, some having an area of hardstanding, and are separated by hedges and mature trees. At the opposite side of the lake from the entrance, there is a separate area for tents with its own sanitary block. The adjoining national park offers a wealth of holiday/sporting activities including walking, cycling (there are two passenger ferries that take cycles), boat trips, cable car and much more. Full details are available at the friendly reception. For winter sports lovers, the ski centre at Winterberg is only 30 km. away from this all-year-round site. With a wide range of facilities for children, this is an ideal family site, as well as being suited to country lovers.

You might like to know

There are some excellent walking areas within the immediate vicinity of the site, including the Kellerwald Edersee National Park.

- ☑ Dogs welcome *(subject to conditions)*
- ☑ Dogs welcome all season
- ○ Dogs welcome part season
- ☑ Breed restrictions *(e.g. only small dogs accepted)*
- ○ Number restrictions *(max. 1 or 2 dogs)*
- ○ Dog sanitary facilities *(e.g. waste bins, bags)*
- ○ Dog showers
- ○ On-site dog walking area
- ○ Kennels
- ○ Vet nearby *(able to help with UK Pet Passports)*

Facilities:
Two excellent sanitary blocks, all heated, clean and well maintained, include many washbasins in cabins and free showers. Facilities for wheelchair users. Family rooms (free). Baby room, superb children's bathroom, child size toilets and washbasins. Laundry facilities. Motorcaravan services. Gas supplies. Small shop (31/3-9/11). Restaurant, snacks and takeaway. New spa centre and swimming pools (outdoor 12/5-9/9, heated indoor all year). TV and club room. Playground. Sauna (free after two night stay). Children's club. Riding. Bicycle and electric car hire. WiFi over site (charged). New log chalets for hire. Off site: Swimming 150 m. ATM in Seelbach 1 km. Riding 1.5 km. Golf 5 km.

Open: All year.

Directions: From A5/E35 autobahn, leave at exit 56 (Lahr). Follow L36/L415 road east through Lahr, until turn south to Seelbach. Go through Seelbach and the site is 1 km. south, on the right.
GPS: 48.29972, 7.94422

Charges guide

Per unit incl. 2 persons and electricity (plus meter) € 31,10 - € 35,10

extra person € 10,90	
child (3-12 yrs) € 8,10	
dog € 3,50	

No credit cards.

Ferienparadies Schwarzwälder Hof

Tretenhofstrasse 76, D-77960 Seelbach (Baden-Württemberg)
t: 078 239 60950   e: info@spacamping.de
alanrogers.com/DE34270   www.spacamping.de

Accommodation: ✔ Pitch   ✔ Mobile home/chalet   ✔ Hotel/B&B   ○ Apartment

This site lies in a wooded valley, just south of the pleasant village of Seelbach in the Black Forest. The old buildings have been replaced by very attractive ones built in traditional log cabin style, but containing very modern facilities. There are 180 well drained touring pitches, either grass or hardstanding, all with electricity (10A Europlug), water supply and waste water outlet. There is also space for groups in tents. Just by the entrance is the family hotel with a restaurant and wellness centre. Besides a comprehensive general menu, there are also menus for children and older people with smaller appetites. Health spa and swimming pools. In July and August a good range of activities are organised for all ages, including a children's club. Fishing for tiddlers is possible in the stream which runs along the bottom of the site. The surrounding countryside is good for walking and cycling, and Europa Park is 30 km.

You might like to know

This site has a first-rate spa and sauna complex, a perfect break from everyday life and stress.

- ✔ Dogs welcome *(subject to conditions)*
- ✔ Dogs welcome all season
- ○ Dogs welcome part season
- ✔ Breed restrictions *(e.g. only small dogs accepted)*
- ✔ Number restrictions *(max. 1 or 2 dogs)*
- ○ Dog sanitary facilities *(e.g. waste bins, bags)*
- ○ Dog showers
- ○ On-site dog walking area
- ○ Kennels
- ✔ Vet nearby *(able to help with UK Pet Passports)*

Gugel's Dreiländer Camping

Oberer Wald 3, D-79395 Neuenburg am Rhein (Baden-Württemberg)
t: 076 317 719   e: info@camping-gugel.de
alanrogers.com/DE34550   www.camping-gugel.de

Accommodation: ☑ Pitch   ☑ Mobile home/chalet   ○ Hotel/B&B   ○ Apartment

Facilities: Three good quality, heated sanitary blocks include some washbasins in cabins. Baby room. Facilities for disabled visitors. Laundry facilities. Motorcaravan services. Shop. Excellent restaurant. Takeaway (weekends and daily in high season). Wellness centre. Indoor/outdoor pool. Community room with TV. Activity programme (high season). Play areas. Boules. Tennis. Fishing. Minigolf. Barbecue. Beach bar. Petting zoo and aviary. Electric go-karts. Bicycle hire. Free WiFi in central area. Off site: Riding 1.5 km. Golf 5 km. Neuenburg, Breisach, Freiburg, Basel and the Black Forest.

Open: All year.

Directions: From autobahn A5 take Neuenburg exit, turn left, then almost immediately left at traffic lights, left at next junction and follow signs for 2 km. to site (called 'Neuenburg' on most signs).
GPS: 47.79693, 7.55

Charges guide

Per unit incl. 2 persons and electricity	€ 26,00
extra person	€ 6,50
child (2-15 yrs)	€ 3,50
dog	€ 3,00

Discount every 10th night.

Set in natural heath and woodland, Gugel's is an attractive site with 220 touring pitches, either in small clearings in the trees, in open areas or on a hardstanding section used for overnight stays. All have electricity (10/16A), and 40 also have water, waste water and satellite TV connections. Opposite is a meadow where late arrivals and early departures may spend the night. There may be some road noise near the entrance. The site may become very busy in high season and on bank holidays but you should always find room. The excellent pool and wellness complex add to the attraction of this all year site. There is a social room with satellite TV where guests are welcomed with a glass of wine and a slide presentation of the attractions of the area. The Rhine is within walking distance and there is an extensive programme of activities on offer for all ages. The site is ideally placed not only for enjoying and exploring the south of the Black Forest, but also for night stops when travelling from Frankfurt to Basel on the A5 autobahn. A doctor is on call.

You might like to know

As well as having green and wooded areas, this site is also the starting point of the Nordic walking course.

- ☑ Dogs welcome *(subject to conditions)*
- ☑ Dogs welcome all season
- ○ Dogs welcome part season
- ○ Breed restrictions *(e.g. only small dogs accepted)*
- ☑ Number restrictions *(max. 1 or 2 dogs)*
- ○ Dog sanitary facilities *(e.g. waste bins, bags)*
- ○ Dog showers
- ○ On-site dog walking area
- ○ Kennels
- ○ Vet nearby *(able to help with UK Pet Passports)*

Camping Romantische Strasse

Munster 67, D-97993 Creglingen-Münster (Baden-Württemberg)
t: 079 332 0289 e: camping.hausotter@web.de
alanrogers.com/DE36020 www.camping-romantische-strasse.de

Accommodation: ☑ Pitch ○ Mobile home/chalet ○ Hotel/B&B ○ Apartment

This popular tourist area can become very busy during summer, and Romantische Strasse will be greatly appreciated for its peaceful situation in a wooded valley just outside the small village of Münster. There are 100 grass touring pitches (out of 140), many level, others with a small degree of slope. They are not hedged or fenced in order to keep the natural appearance of the woodland. All the pitches have electricity (6A), some shade, and are situated either side of a stream (fenced off from a weir at the far end of the site). Twenty-seven fully serviced pitches are on higher ground near reception. Having already built a new reception, renovated the pool, sauna, solarium and changing rooms, and made an open-air chess and boules area, the friendly, English-speaking owners are looking to further develop the area by the lake. The village of Münster is on a scenic road just 3 km. from Creglingen and the 100 km. long Tauber valley cycle route, and about 16 km. from the beautiful town of Rothenburg on the Tauber which is very popular in high season.

You might like to know

A number of accompanied walks are arranged on a regular basis, including excursions to Ullrichskapelle and Rothenburger Landhege.

- ☑ Dogs welcome *(subject to conditions)*
- ☑ Dogs welcome all season
- ○ Dogs welcome part season
- ☑ Breed restrictions *(e.g. only small dogs accepted)*
- ☑ Number restrictions *(max. 1 or 2 dogs)*
- ○ Dog sanitary facilities *(e.g. waste bins, bags)*
- ○ Dog showers
- ○ On-site dog walking area
- ○ Kennels
- ○ Vet nearby *(able to help with UK Pet Passports)*

Facilities: The two main sanitary blocks are of good quality with free hot water. A third unit further into the site is due for refurbishment. Launderette. Motorcaravan services. Small shop. Gas supplies. Large, pleasant bar/restaurant at the entrance (1/4-9/11, closed Mon). Barbecue and covered sitting area. Heated indoor swimming pool (caps required) and sauna. Minigolf. Play area. Bicycle hire. Four mobile homes for hire. WiFi (charged). Off site: Bus service 200 m. Large lakes for swimming 100 m. and fishing 500 m. Riding 3.5 km. Rothenburg with its fortifications 16 km.

Open: 15 March - 15 November.

Directions: From the Romantische Strasse between Rothenburg and Bad Mergentheim, exit at Creglingen to Münster (3 km). Site is just beyond this village.
GPS: 49.43950, 10.04211

Charges guide

Per unit incl. 2 persons and electricity	€ 19,90 - € 22,70
extra person	€ 5,50 - € 6,50
child (3-14 yrs)	€ 3,50 - € 4,00
dog	€ 1,00

No credit cards.

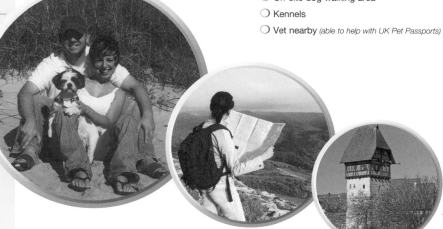

Kur-Gutshof-Camping Arterhof

Hauptstrasse 3, Lengham, D-84364 Bad Birnbach (Bavaria (S))
t: 085 639 6130   e: info@arterhof.de
alanrogers.com/DE36960   www.arterhof.de

Accommodation: ☑ Pitch   ☑ Mobile home/chalet   ○ Hotel/B&B   ○ Apartment

Based around a Bavarian farmstead, Arterhof is an excellent site combining the charm of the old together with the comfort of the new. An attractive courtyard at the front of the site houses reception, a farm shop and a café with a terrace. To the rear is a tropical indoor pool containing soft water at a comfortable 30ºC as well as a sauna, solarium, fitness room and much more. The 190 touring pitches with some hedge separation, on grass or pebble standing, all have TV, electricity, fresh and waste water connections, and 12 have their own pitch-side sanitary facilities. For winter camping, 50 of the pitches have a gas supply. Opposite the site entrance is Inattura, a spacious flower-filled meadow with a large, natural pool, scented garden and lots of lawn; ideal for quiet relaxation and sunbathing in the open Bavarian countryside. There are numerous fitness programmes to cure one's present aches and pains, as well as preventative programmes. With ample provision for children, both outdoor and traditional indoor restaurants, this is a site to suit the whole family.

You might like to know

In addition to an extensive spa and swimming pool complex, this site has an outdoor swimming lake. Trail maps are available from reception to explore the area on foot.

- ☑ Dogs welcome *(subject to conditions)*
- ☑ Dogs welcome all season
- ○ Dogs welcome part season
- ○ Breed restrictions *(e.g. only small dogs accepted)*
- ☑ Number restrictions *(max. 1 or 2 dogs)*
- ○ Dog sanitary facilities *(e.g. waste bins, bags)*
- ○ Dog showers
- ○ On-site dog walking area
- ○ Kennels
- ○ Vet nearby *(able to help with UK Pet Passports)*

Facilities: Modern, attractive, well maintained sanitary blocks with heated floor, free showers, washbasins in cabins, hairdryers and bathrooms to rent. Hairdressing salon, cosmetic studio. Laundry facilities. Motorcaravan service point. Swimming pools. Wellness centre. Traditional restaurant serving southern Bavarian dishes with meat from the farm's own Aberdeen Angus cattle. Play area. Live music Fridays. WiFi. Off site: Rottal Thermal baths in Bad Birnbach (free bus from site). Cycle and mountain bike tracks. Nordic walking. Golf.

Open: All year.

Directions: Site is 12 km. east of Pfarrkirchen. Leave autobahn 3 at exit 106 and head south on B20 to Eggenfelden then east on B20 past Pfarrkirchen to Bad Birnbach where site is signed to the right opposite supermarket.

GPS: 48.435176, 13.109415

Charges guide

Per unit incl. 2 persons and electricity (plus meter)	€ 24,30 - € 28,30
extra person	€ 7,70
child (2-13 yrs)	€ 4,80
dog	€ 2,50

Facilities:
Facilities: Excellent sanitary facilities include private cabins and free showers, facilities for disabled visitors, special child facilities and a dog shower. Two private bathrooms for rent. Laundry facilities. Bar/restaurant. Motorcaravan services. Shop. Gym. Luxury leisure complex (heated outdoor pool 1/3-15/11, indoor pool and wellness all year). Play area. Bicycle hire. Fishing. Internet. WiFi. No charcoal barbecues. Off site: Riding. Fishing.

Open: All year.

Directions: Site is 25 km. southwest of Passau. From A3 take exit 118 and follow signs for Pocking. After 2 km. turn right on B388. Site is in the hamlet of Singham. Turn right into Karpfhan then left towards site.

GPS: 48.42001, 13.19261

Charges guide

Per unit incl. 2 persons
and electricity € 26,10 - € 31,20

extra person € 7,60	
child (0-14 yrs) € 4,80	
dog € 2,50	

Germany – Bad Griesbach

Kur & Feriencamping Dreiquellenbad

Singham 40, D-94086 Bad Griesbach (Bavaria (S))
t: 085 329 6130 e: info@camping-bad-griesbach.de
alanrogers.com/DE36970 www.camping-bad-griesbach.de

Accommodation: ⊘ Pitch ⊘ Mobile home/chalet ○ Hotel/B&B ○ Apartment

This excellent site is part of a wellness, health and beauty spa complex where camping guests have free use of the indoor and outdoor thermal pools, sauna, Turkish bath and jacuzzi. A large selection of treatments are also available (on payment) and the complex has its own doctor. The site has 200 pitches, all with fresh and waste water, electricity and TV connections. In addition, there is a new camping car area (29 units) with its own service point. This is a site where visitors should take full advantage of the facilities, and plenty of information is available at the helpful English-speaking reception. The site's location enables you to combine a relaxing holiday with interesting sightseeing. Regensburg, Munich, Linz and Salzburg are all within easy reach, as is Passau, which dates from Roman times and is where three rivers join to become the Danube, flowing on to the Black Sea. Passau with its cathedral, old town and the peninsula where the Danube and Inn merge are worth visiting. Adjoining the site is Europe's largest golf centre. A member of Leading Campings group.

You might like to know

There are some excellent thermal spa and wellness facilities within easy walking distance of this site.

- ⊘ Dogs welcome *(subject to conditions)*
- ⊘ Dogs welcome all season
- ○ Dogs welcome part season
- ○ Breed restrictions *(e.g. only small dogs accepted)*
- ⊘ Number restrictions *(max. 1 or 2 dogs)*
- ○ Dog sanitary facilities *(e.g. waste bins, bags)*
- ⊘ Dog showers
- ○ On-site dog walking area
- ○ Kennels
- ○ Vet nearby *(able to help with UK Pet Passports)*

Facilities: Two good sanitary blocks near the entrance and another modern block next to the hotel, both include toilets, washbasins and spacious, controllable showers (on payment). Child size toilets and baby room. Toilet for disabled visitors. Sauna and massage. Launderette with sinks, hot water and a washing machine. Shop (15/6-15/9). Bar/snack bar with pool table. Games room. Swimming pool (6x12 m). Adventure style playground on grass with climbing wall. Trampolines. Tennis. Minigolf. Archery. Russian bowling. Paragliding. Rock climbing. Bicycle hire. Entertainment programme. Excursions to Prague.
Off site: Fishing and beach 800 m. Riding 2 km. Golf 5 km.

Open: All year.

Directions: Follow road no. 14 from Liberec to Vrchlabi. At the roundabout turn towards Prague and site is 1.5 km. on the right.

GPS: 50.61036, 15.60264

Charges guide

Per unit incl. 2 persons and electricity	CZK 294 - 390
extra person	CZK 55 - 65
child (4-15 yrs)	CZK 38 - 45
dog	CZK 45 - 50

Various discounts available in low season.

Holiday Park Lisci Farma

Dolni Branna 350, CZ-54362 Vrchlabi (Vychodocesky)
t: 499 421 473 e: info@liscifarma.cz
alanrogers.com/CZ4590 www.liscifarma.cz

Accommodation: ☑ Pitch ☑ Mobile home/chalet ○ Hotel/B&B ○ Apartment

This is truly an excellent site that could be in Western Europe considering its amenities, pitches and welcome. However, Lisci Farma retains a pleasant Czech atmosphere. In the winter months, when local skiing is available, snow chains are essential. The 260 pitches are fairly flat, although the terrain is slightly sloping and some pitches are terraced. There is shade and some pitches have hardstanding. A beautiful sandy, lakeside beach is 800 m. from the entrance. The site is well equipped for the whole family with its adventure playground with trampolines, archery, beach volleyball, Russian bowling and an outdoor bowling court. The more active can go paragliding or rock climbing, with experienced people to guide you. Excursions to Prague are organised and, if all the sporting possibilities are not enough, the children can take part in the activities of the entertainment team, while you are walking or cycling or enjoying live music at the Fox Saloon. The site reports the addition of completely new electrical connections, restaurant, games room and mini-market.

You might like to know

This site is open all year – a good choice for a winter break for you and your dog?

- ☑ Dogs welcome *(subject to conditions)*
- ☑ Dogs welcome all season
- ○ Dogs welcome part season
- ○ Breed restrictions *(e.g. only small dogs accepted)*
- ☑ Number restrictions *(max. 1 or 2 dogs)*
- ○ Dog sanitary facilities *(e.g. waste bins, bags)*
- ○ Dog showers
- ○ On-site dog walking area
- ○ Kennels
- ○ Vet nearby *(able to help with UK Pet Passports)*

Facilities: Three immaculate toilet blocks with washbasins, preset showers (charged) and an en-suite bathroom with toilet, basin and shower. Facilities for disabled visitors. Launderette. Shop, restaurant and bar, takeaway (1/5-15/9). Motorcaravan services. Playground. Canoe, bicycle, pedalos, rowing boat and surfboard hire. Kidstown. Volleyball competitions. Rafting. Bus trips to Prague. Torches useful. Internet access and WiFi. Off site: Shops and restaurants in the village 900 m. from reception. Golf 7 km. Riding 15 km.

Open: 25 April - 21 September.

Directions: Take exit 114 at Passau in Germany (near Austrian border) towards Freyung in Czech Republic. Continue to Philipsreut, from there follow the no. 4 road towards Vimperk. Turn right a few kilometres after border towards Volary on no. 141 road. From Volary follow the no. 163 road to Horni Plana, Cerna and Frymburk. Site is on 163 road, right after village.

GPS: 48.655947, 14.170239

Charges guide

Per unit incl. 2 persons
and electricity CZK 460 - 810

extra person CZK 80 - 130

child (2-11 yrs) CZK 60 - 90

dog CZK 50 - 60

No credit cards.

Czech Republic – Frymburk

Camping Frymburk

Frymburk 184, CZ-38279 Frymburk (Jihocesky)
t: 380 735 284 e: info@campingfrymburk.cz
alanrogers.com/CZ4720 www.campingfrymburk.cz

Accommodation: ☑ Pitch ☑ Mobile home/chalet ○ Hotel/B&B ○ Apartment

Camping Frymburk is beautifully located on the Lipno lake in southern Bohemia and is an ideal site. From this site, activities could include walking, cycling, swimming, sailing, canoeing or rowing, and afterwards you could relax in the small, cosy bar/restaurant. You could enjoy a real Czech meal in one of the restaurants in Frymburk or on site. The site has 170 level pitches on terraces (all with 6A electricity, some with hardstanding and four have private sanitary units) and from the lower terraces on the edge of the lake there are lovely views over the water to the woods on the opposite side. A ferry crosses the lake from Frymburk where one can walk or cycle in the woods. The Dutch owner, Mr Wilzing, will welcome the whole family, personally siting your caravan. Children will be entertained by 'Kidstown' and the site has a small beach.

You might like to know

South Bohemia (Sumava) is the largest protected, natural area in the Czech Republic and consists of a range of mountains, 120 km. long, and countless opportunities for excellent walking.

☑ Dogs welcome *(subject to conditions)*

☑ Dogs welcome all season

○ Dogs welcome part season

☑ Breed restrictions *(e.g. only small dogs accepted)*

☑ Number restrictions *(max. 1 or 2 dogs)*

○ Dog sanitary facilities *(e.g. waste bins, bags)*

○ Dog showers

○ On-site dog walking area

○ Kennels

○ Vet nearby *(able to help with UK Pet Passports)*

Camping Pension Kolodeje

CZ-37501 Kolodeje nad Luznici (Jihocesky)
t: 737 782 725   e: info@campingkolodeje.eu
alanrogers.com/CZ4768 www.campingkolodeje.eu

Accommodation: ⊘ Pitch ⊘ Mobile home/chalet ⊘ Hotel/B&B ○ Apartment

Facilities: Central sanitary facility. Restaurant, social room/bar with terrace. Fresh bread every morning. River swimming. Fishing. Canoes, rowing boat and mountain bikes to rent (July/Aug). Internet (July/Aug). Off site: Shop 200 m. for groceries, larger shops and restaurants 3 km. Walking and cycling routes close. Tyn nad Vltavou 3 km. Riding 5 km. Hluboka castle 20 km. Zoo 20 km. Ceské Boudovice 25 km. Prague 110 km.

Open: 1 June - 1 September.

Directions: Site is 36 km. north of Ceske Budejovice. From Tyn nad Vltavou take 105 towards Milevsko for 3 km. At Kolodeje cross the bridge and site is on right.

GPS: 49.25426, 14.419979

Charges guide

Per unit incl. 2 persons and electricity	CZK 400
dog (one free) no charge -	CZK 40

This small, peaceful, rural site is located in South Bohemia and is situated by the River Luznici, next to the small village of Kolodeje nad Luznici. There are 50 touring pitches, all with 10A electricity, together with 5 hiking cabins, 1 house and several caravans to rent. The pitches are dispersed throughout the site, are fairly open and some have a little shade from the trees. The field next to the river is both a place for relaxation and a starting point for river swimming and other water activities. There are plenty of opportunities for walking, hiking and mountain biking with many tracks and paths very close to the site. In addition, Kolodeje is well placed to visit the surrounding towns and castles, including Prague (110 km). Ronald and Liesbeth organise special weekly packages in June to explore the history and culture of the Czech Republic. The package includes tours, regional food and local crafts.

You might like to know

Camping Kolodeje is the ideal place for camping with your dog, whether swimming in the river or enjoying long walks through the forest. The first dog stays free of charge.

- ⊘ Dogs welcome *(subject to conditions)*
- ⊘ Dogs welcome all season
- ○ Dogs welcome part season
- ○ Breed restrictions *(e.g. only small dogs accepted)*
- ⊘ Number restrictions *(max. 1 or 2 dogs)*
- ○ Dog sanitary facilities *(e.g. waste bins, bags)*
- ○ Dog showers
- ⊘ On-site dog walking area
- ⊘ Kennels
- ⊘ Vet nearby *(able to help with UK Pet Passports)*

Facilities: Modern and comfortable toilet facilities provide British style toilets, open washbasins (cold water only) and free, controllable hot showers. Campers' kitchen. Bar/restaurant with one meal served daily. Play area. Tennis. Minigolf. Riding. Some live music nights in high season. Internet and WiFi (charged). Only gas and electric barbecues allowed on pitches. Tours to Vienna, Brno and wine cellars organised. Torch useful. Off site: Fishing and boat launching 2 km. Beach 10 km.

Open: 1 May - 31 October.

Directions: Coming from the northwest on the E59 road exit to the east at Kasarna onto the 408 road and continue north on the 361 road towards Hluboke Masuvky. Site is well signed.

GPS: 48.9192, 16.0256

Charges guide

Per unit incl. 2 persons and electricity CZK 470	
extra person CZK 120	
child (3-12 yrs) CZK 60	
dog CZK 50	

Czech Republic – Hluboke Masuvky

Camping Country

Hluboke Masuvky 257, CZ-67152 Hluboke Masuvky (Jihomoravsky)
t: 515 255 249   e: camping-country@cbox.cz
alanrogers.com/CZ4896   www.camp-country.com

Accommodation: ◉ Pitch ◉ Mobile home/chalet ○ Hotel/B&B ○ Apartment

Camping Country is a well cared for and attractively landscaped site close to the historical town of Znojmo. It is a rural location, in a wine growing region close to a national park, and with its small wine cellar, wine tasting evenings, small stables and riding school, barbecue and campfire areas, is an ideal site for a longer stay. Visitors will enjoy the new cycling routes which have been set out in the national park. Camping Country has 50 pitches (all for tourers), 30 with 16A electricity, on two fields – one behind the main house taking six or eight units, the other one larger with a gravel access road. The fields are connected by two wooden bridges (one is only fenced on one side). Varieties of low hedges and firs partly separate the pitches. To the front of the site is a paddock with two horses and facilities for minigolf, volleyball, basketball and tennis. In the garden of the main house is a paddling pool. Colourful flowers and trees give the site a pleasant atmosphere.

You might like to know

As its name suggests, Camping Country is a great site for exploring the Czech countryside – maybe the national nature reserve at Podyji, or castles in Vranov or Bitov.

- ◉ Dogs welcome *(subject to conditions)*
- ◉ Dogs welcome all season
- ○ Dogs welcome part season
- ○ Breed restrictions *(e.g. only small dogs accepted)*
- ◉ Number restrictions *(max. 1 or 2 dogs)*
- ○ Dog sanitary facilities *(e.g. waste bins, bags)*
- ○ Dog showers
- ○ On-site dog walking area
- ○ Kennels
- ○ Vet nearby *(able to help with UK Pet Passports)*

Been to any good campsites lately?
We have

You'll find them here...

... also here...

101 great campsites, ideal for your specific hobby, pastime or passion

Want independent campsite reviews at your fingertips?

You'll find them here...

Over 3,000 in-depth campsite reviews at **www.alanrogers.com**

...and even here...

FREE Alan Rogers bookstore app
- digital editions of all 2014 guides
alanrogers.com/digital

An exciting free app from iTunes
the Apple app store

Want to book your holiday on one of Europe's top campsites?

We can do it for you. No problem.

The best campsites in the most popular regions - we'll take care of everything

alan rogers ⬤ travel

Discover the best campsites in Europe
with Alan Rogers

alanrogers.com
01580 214000

Index

Index

Index